RYAN GANDER

Ampersand

Notes on a collection

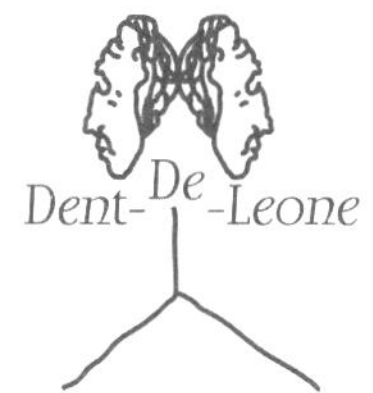

“Like trying to graffiti on the Death Star”
Miranda Sawyer

For Rebecca...
a bit.

Ampersand — Notes on a collection
Ryan Gander

Written by Ryan Gander
Edited by Rebecca May Marston with Phil Mayer
Transcription and proof-reading by Barnie Page
Photography by Ryan Gander and John Newton

Design by Åbäke with Line Monthiers
Printed by die Keure, Bruges, Belgium
Published by Dent-De-Leone, 2012
www.dentdeleone.co.nz

'Mr Playlist' was first published as 'The Atelier' in *freefall: Arts Council England International Artists Fellowships 2001 – 2003*, Arts Council England, 2004.
'Rietveld's Pieces' was first published in *Appendix Appendix*, Ryan Gander and Stuart Bailey, Christoph Keller Editions, 2007.
'Saddle' was first published as 'Being van Doesburg' in *In My View: Personal Reflections on Art by Today's Leading Artists*, Simon Grant, Thames & Hudson, 2012.
'Seeds' was first published as *Mostly English; not too English*, T.E. White, Franco Fitzpatrick, 2011, on the occasion of 'Locked Room Scenario' (2011), Ryan Gander, an Artangel commission.
Elements of 'Smoked Vodka' appeared in *Artists' Cocktails Here*, Ryan Gander and Mario Garcia Torres on the occasion of dOCUMENTA (13), 2012.
'The Sitting' was previously published as part of 'Announcement for the book *The Sitting*' (2009), Ryan Gander.

ISBN: 978-1-907908-08-8

Published with the support of Tokyo Arts Club, Paris.

Foreword to the fifth edition.

FOREWORD

Can the fifth edition ever be published before the third? Can this book be both a prelude and a sequel to an exhibition? Did you ever notice the word ampers& contains itself? Esperlu&te aussi? Did you know Roland Barthes' *Empire of Signs* is apparently best read if one is born and raised in France but of Japanese descent?

Ryan Gander and I were once in a lift of a hotel in Tokyo when we noticed the absence of a button for the 13th floor. Despite our amusement at the superstitious gesture we later suggested at the front desk that they should have built the 13th floor, but prohibited access to it. An architectural ghost in need of physicality to truly abolish bad omens.

The present publication crystallises, for a fleeting moment (books are not eternal, you know), the ever expanding collection of Ryan Gander and the stories for which objects of all pedigree – artworks alongside coloured toilet paper – are the catalysts of. These short essays are an exploration of our surroundings, both normal and sublime, written with a steady hand and the sharp critical eye of a northern comedian cooler than Pharrell Williams. You think I go too far? I am so sincere I am not even paid to write this foreword.

Maki Suzuki, 2012

CONTENTS

A fresh baguette purchased daily from the boulangerie nearest to the exhibition venue.

Years ago whilst staying with a friend in Paris it was explained to me that every bakery in France, no matter how posh the neighbourhood nor how well crafted their artisan bread, was obliged by law to sell a certain number of standard baguettes at a low, fixed price. This is a governmental attempt to make sure that no-one goes hungry, irrespective of class and income. I'm not sure that humans can exist on bread alone, but the notion has a generous civic intention that cannot be underestimated.

It's interesting that in the UK the baguette (which for so long we have called 'French bread' or a 'French stick', reinforcing our need to identify otherness) is seen as a luxury item. It's more commonplace now, but I remember vivid scenes from the '80s of my parents, every Saturday morning in the kitchen of our suburban home, celebrating the fact that following our visit to Sainsbury's we would eat a chicken sandwich made from a real 'French stick'. The 'French stick' was not the ideal bread for sandwich making, but we grimaced through the pain of the hard crust cutting our gums and spiking the roofs of our mouths. It was nice to know that this 'unusual' bread represented not the basic staple food distributed to the starving, but something really quite exotic.

PALAIS DE TOKYO RUIN

A clay model, handmade by the artist, intended to represent the Palais de Tokyo as a ruin at some future moment.

Strangely intrigued by incomplete things, I keep a collection of images of both partially built and partially destroyed buildings. In 2010 I conceived a work that combined this interest along with my obsession for para-possible realities and the consequences of decision making; I made a scale model of Renzo Piano's glass-bricked building, Maison Hermès (2001), in Toyko, but as a ruin from the year 2032. It merged architectural feat and the failure of Modernism – a trajectory poignant to a few investigations within my practice. The model was to be shown in an exhibition I had been invited to present at the Hermès Foundation, housed within the Maison Hermès building. My exhibition was scheduled for June 2011, which came to fall three months after the disastrous Miyagi earthquake and subsequent nuclear power station meltdown that affected the whole of Japan. With temporarily disabled electrical energy production the government put restrictions on domestic, commercial and industrial power consumption. Maison Hermès could not function as an exhibition space throughout the summer of 2011 because it was impossible to light and air condition the three gallery floors. The show was postponed until later in the year, at which time I thought it appropriate to remove my ruined building model from the show. It would have been insensitive and too evocative of the widespread destruction and loss of life that Miyagi caused.

I think the beauty of a model ruin lies not only in the way it prompts us to imagine the circumstances leading to such devastating consequences, but also in the way it allows us to see within a microcosm, which one usually associates with an idealised view of reality. As a child I was deeply intrigued by any sort of model in which it was possible to peer through windows and doors into an inaccessible interior space. The catalyst to imagine myself within this micro-reality was deeply fascinating. A model ruin acts in the same way; it gives us the ability to map a floor plan and speculate the divisions and functions of spaces, catapulting our imaginations into overdrive. The unshown Maison Hermès model sits in a box in my cellar in Suffolk, like an untruthful time capsule waiting to be rediscovered.

JOBS' KEYBOARD

An Apple keyboard purposely defaced and autographed by Steve Jobs.

I've read many times in many places that Steve Jobs, the late CEO and co-founder of Apple Inc., was a difficult man. His behaviour seemed selfish and antisocial, almost autistic. He was ruthlessly demanding to work with, obsessed with simplicity of design and the eradication of the frivolous and unnecessary. He was also desperate for control, for his own input to be manifest, and for a legacy that lived up to his vision. It was unspoken, but known, that Jobs' personal stylistic signature had to be present in every output of the company.

At the age of 30 Jobs was fired by his own board for his erratic and irrational behaviour, but on his return to Apple Inc. almost a decade later, when he became the head of the company once again, an incredible scene occurred in a design workshop at Apple Inc. headquarters in Cupertino, USA. Presented with a keyboard to review (which had been produced during his ten year absence) Jobs pulled his car keys from his pocket and began mutilating it. Violently, he broke off all the keys that were not present on the keyboard he himself had designed a decade earlier – the keys which, in his absence, his successors had reinstated to make the Mac more like a Microsoft PC (namely the function and cursor keys). When he had finished he took out a marker pen and signed the keyboard, announcing: "I'm changing the world one keyboard at a time."

CUBS HAT

A rare, vintage, short-peaked baseball cap, on which the 'C' symbol of the Chicago Cubs American baseball team is embroidered.

About a year ago I took to wearing a baseball cap, which would have been unimaginable to me only a few years before. The types of baseball caps I wear, of which I now have a substantial collection, are the high-topped variants with a very straight, flat peak, like the ones American hip-hop stars wear. In the beginning I wore them with a sense of irony: a white, middle-class, specky-four-eyes, relatively affluent, at times intellectual, family man sporting a recognisable signifier of a different ilk and genre. But after a year of wearing these baseball caps they've become part of my persona, or new persona. I rarely leave the house without a hat and I've managed to collect many from all over the world. The markings and logos on caps that suggest legacy, history, geography and cultural or social significance have become a distracting preoccupation.

One of my favourite hats is the first hat that I bought whilst lecturing in Chicago.[1] The hat is a royal blue colour embroidered with a very simple red 'C' with a white outline, possibly from the typeface Gill Sans. Obviously the 'C' represents the 'C' of the Cubs, one of the two major baseball teams from Chicago, the other being the White Sox.

1. Another personal favourite is a hat I purchased in Japan for the Tokyo baseball team The Swallows, renamed Tokyo Yakult Swallows to acknowledge their main sponsor in 2006. The logo is a play on the 'Y' and 'S' characters in the Westernised character set. A mergence of the two Western characters that also resembles the Chinese Kanji[2] sign 'Lihei' translat-

ing to 'strength' or 'power'. This collision of a Chinese Kanji and a Western Latin character set – of two cultures and two languages – results coincidentally in a reversed right facing Swastika type logo (those which were used during the Second World War as a symbol for the Nazi Party). In opposition to the Swastika's signification, the left facing variant of the symbol is a tantric symbol to evoke 'shakti', the sacred symbol of auspiciousness (one of the most prominent spiritual symbols in Hinduism, Jainism and Buddhism, found adorning temples and religious shrines throughout Asia).

2. The adopted logographic Chinese characters (hanzi) used in the modern Japanese writing system.

What appeals to me about this hat is its ability to represent dual meaning as it crosses the Atlantic. The same red 'C' logo exists in British culture in a subsection of Transport for London – the Congestion Charge (a penalty for those driving within central London). When I'm in the US and happen to be wearing the hat I am greeted with: "Hey man, are you a Cubs fan?" / "Great team dude" / "Cubs! Cubs! Cubs!" When I'm driving in my car in London (an estate car that could quite equally be driven by a Congestion Charge official as much as anyone else) I receive wary double glances. Of course this collision of meaning and graphics is entirely coincidental, but it's hard to ignore the beauty of such happenstance as it dances nimbly through your mind, tongue-in-cheek, light on its feet, with a wry little smile.

A firework rocket.

One of the most memorable lessons I learned as a teenager in physics class was the relationship between potential and kinetic energy. From the glossaries that haunt the backs of contemporary art books we know that Kinetic Art made a significant contribution to the landscape of 20th century art. And so what of the potential?

Every year I encounter at least three or four titles by art historians and futurologists (admittedly usually in airport bookshops – a context where certainty is craved to balance the uncertainty of air travel) that attempt to speculate the next big movement in both contemporary art and the world at large. An impossible objective, and in many respects a totally pointless one. The trajectory of trending in the history of contemporary art cannot be traced; it is an activity that is fuelled by uncertainty, whim, counter-movement and action against the mainstream.

The ambiguity of potentiality is the motivation that drives me; the unknowing, the transience and the indeterminable trajectories of art are the very things in which I find pleasure. It is charming and romantic to sit on a beach and gaze at eruptions of fireworks overhead, but the expectation of the lit fuse is more relative to the practice of everyday life. There is something to be said for 'making of it what you will'. Allowing space for the imagination to play and skip freely requires a resistance of closure, for the ending of the story not to be revealed, to hint at a catalyst of imminent kinetics, but for it to always remain as potential. This in order that the kinetic manifests itself in our imaginations in every possibility; in a multitude of colours and a vast array of bleeps and tweets of differing sounds that we choose for ourselves.

A collection of objects used to make the Foley sounds which provide the background noises (such as creaks, rustles and footsteps), in real-time, during the performance of dramatic plays for radio.

SOUND EFFECT PROPS

Kkkrridddttttkk

Klick
klock
Klick
klock
Klick
klock

B
r
r
r
r
r
r
r
r
r
i
i
i
i
i
i
i
i
i
i
i
i
i
n
g

Crreeeeeeeeaaak

SLA A AM

E-E-E-E-u-r-g-h-h-h-----.

PILE OF LEAVES

A pile of one hundred artificial autumn leaves produced in China by the company Fall Accents.

The development of coded language in semi-private circles is commonplace. Anthropologically people who congregate around common activities, themes and perspectives, not only dress and behave similarly, but also produce new words and language that can describe things more economically and poignantly. One of the greatest examples of this is 'Cockney rhyming slang', developed in the 1800s in London's East End by market stall traders who needed a codified language to communicate with one another without customers understanding, for example about profit margins when marking up the cost of produce. In another example Erving Goffman cites a 'backstage language of behaviour' primarily in British football terrace culture:

> *Throughout western society there tends to be one informal or backstage language of behaviour, and another language of behaviour for occasions when a performance is being presented. The backstage language of behaviour consists of reciprocal first-naming, cooperative decision making, profanity, open sexual remarks, elaborate griping, smoking, rough informal dress, sloppy sitting and standing postures, use of dialect or substandard speech,*

mumbling and shouting, playful aggressiveness and kidding, inconsiderateness for the other in minor but potentially inconsiderate acts, minor physical self involvements such as humming, whistling, chewing, nibbling, belching and flatulence.[1]

1. Erving Goffman, *The Presentation of Self in Everyday Life*, Doubleday, 1959, p. 128.

Many of the above are traits now highly visible and prevalent in all contemporary subcultures: from art students to cycle couriers, film industry professionals to aerobics class participants. In my studio there is a form of this backstage language of behaviour; as time passes and we develop a greater understanding of each other's personalities and as our archive of shared experiences grows, so our inside communications become more intricate and complex. I noticed it recently when a friend came to the studio for lunch and said that they didn't understand half of the things we talked about.

The origins of one of our shorthand terms came from an exacting example: one day I was looking at a work I'd recently had fabricated and said to Phil, my studio manager: "Does it look worn enough? Like we found it as opposed to having it fabricated?" He replied: "It's hard to tell because I've spent so much time with it, but maybe we could get some leaves and rub them on the wood on the top to make it look a bit more worn and perhaps sprinkle the remnants of the leaves and some litter around the side of it on the gallery floor to make it look like it's been brought in from outside?" I said: "That's a great idea!" For us 'adding leaves' now describes the crucial dichotomy of the staged and the un-staged within works. We mean a conceptual adding of leaves to an artwork in production, something to make it seem less like a charged objet d'art and more something that has fallen naturally from the world into a gallery. In my view within the making of contemporary art there is an incredibly fine balance between the finished and the unfinished, the over-produced and the under-produced, the seesaw between objets d'art and objets du monde. It's subtle and there are very few words to communicate the sliding balance between these polarities.

Phil says: "It looks a bit like it's just come out of the foundry, do you think it needs scuffing up a bit?" I reply: "Yeah, more leaves Phil." John replies: "Leaves." Barnie replies: "Leaves." Ann-Marie replies: "Leaves!"

Yeah, leaves.

A JVC HX-D77J Mini System incorporating radio, compact disc and USB input port, which is no longer in production.

The JVC HX-D77J personal stereo system is a brilliant, though unintentional, example of translation of function, specifically a translation from the audible to the visual. Visually I find this piece of audio equipment grotesque and obscene. It lacks almost every quality a product designer would aspire to: subtlety, intelligence, humour, cultural knowing, historical recognition, beauty and charisma. There is, however, a heavy-handed suggestion that the function of this piece of equipment is singular: to play aggressive music at a high volume. A product of an '80s trend for barbarically loud music that is superbly illustrated in Maxell's famous advert in which a man seated on a Le Corbusier LC2 chair is swept backwards by the sheer force emitted from his stereo system. It was a trend that didn't survive because the cost of producing high volume, high definition sound was too expensive for the majority of the consumer market. Slowly, surely and in complete contradiction, audio devices were shrunk down into small, sleek, stylised, pocketable boxes with headphones.

The moment a spectator lays their eyes upon the JVC HX-D77J an image of its user is conjured (albeit built on a stereotype) of a Lynx deodorant-wearing teenage boy, whose taste is based on what is new in a mail-order catalogue. I love this ridiculous stereo system because it reminds me of the gaps between listening and looking. When you are confronted by any visual object you have the ability to close your eyes or look at something else. In fact, most objects like this stereo system consume less than 10% of a our field of vision when being directly looked at. Comparatively it is usually impossible to shut out sound, most sound consumes 100% of our audible landscape. It is possible to put your fingers in your ears to try and block something out, but that restricts the reception of all other audible information. The beauty of the JVC HX-D77J is that it is as much designed and built for the sighted[1] as it is designed and built for the listener. Its function becomes twofold. With all of its boisterous flaws it succeeds in communicating (or at the very least suggesting) the type of music that it has been designed to play. Just as I would speculate that a leather and brass-clad, pseudo-vintage Roberts DAB Radio is more often than not tuned into BBC Radio 2, 3, 4 or Classic FM. The perfect cultural collision or contradiction[2] would be to encounter a JVC HX-D77J blasting out Vaughan Williams.

1. 'The sighted' is a phrase frequently used by Alighiero Boetti, but was invented by blind Braille readers to describe the population of those who are able to see.

2. For years I have attempted to develop a word to describe the types of cultural collisions and contradictions that make the pursuit of being a phenomenologist an absolute pleasure. Without success. Recommendations are welcome on a postcard: The Grand National, PO BOX 48746, London E1 8WX, UK.

REBECCA'S BLANKET

A blanket made for the artist by his wife from recycled woollen jumpers and cardigans found in charity shops local to the town in which they live.

Last year for Christmas my wife gave me a blanket. She made it by hand from recycled jumpers, labouring for endless hours in front of the fire, on the cold, dark winter evenings whilst I was away at work. The blanket is made of numerous assorted woollen golfing cardigans, outdoorsy woollen sweaters and cricket jumpers, all cut up then sewn together; a mismatch of patterns, colours, logos, pockets, hems and buttons. Of course the object holds value for me on a number of levels: its association with being a Christmas gift, the fact it was gifted to me by a loved one, the notion that it's intended to provide warmth on the same sofa on which it was made, and the fact it was produced by hand – a labour-intensive act of love. Furthermore, its appearance clearly tells all these stories; its subconscious showiness tells the viewer a back-story of nostalgia, romanticism and love.

Another value of the blanket is economy of means. It unwittingly reminds one of a vast array of recycling associated crafts: from the cobbling together of remnants of worn out textiles in the tradition of Dutch patchwork and quilt making, to the 'making do and getting by' genre of contemporary desert dwellers.[1] When I use this blanket, on occasion a tune comes to mind from my childhood: the theme tune of the children's animation *The Wombles*. Created by author Elisabeth Beresford, Wombles were a breed of fictional, pointy-nosed, furry creatures that lived in burrows on Wimbledon Common in London, UK. They aimed to help the environment by collecting and recycling rubbish in creative ways. With that theme tune rolling around my mind, I am visited by a wave of nostalgia and romanticism. A romanticism I manipulatively alluded to in the opening lines: "…labouring for endless hours in front of the fire, on the cold, dark winter evenings whilst I was away at work." A romanticism that is greater than the coverage of the blanket, and an affection warmer than its thermal abilities.

1. Those who build vast communities based on lateral thinking, who ingeniously adapt found objects into useful tools, furniture and structures, such as the communes in Arcosanti, Arizona, USA or Auroville, Pondicherry, India.

SEEDS

A large cylindrical glass vase, half-filled with a mixture of various carnivorous plants seeds, which, when fully grown, consume other plants and insects.

When the knife slips between my ribs, I initially think it's an accident, then after a few moments I realise it is intentional. Intentional, but perhaps a blunder? Mistaken identity. I don't see my assailant. It's crowded outside the bar, but everything is calm, no screams, no one even notices anything abnormal. I stumble away. I know I am wounded, but not fatally. I drop my weight back into the car seat, take the keys out of my coat pocket and slowly drive east. I light a cigarette as I queue for the slip road onto The Highway. It isn't until I reach Leiston that I realise how bad it is. As I approach the house it's dawn. I turn off the headlights on the car at the end of the drive, take it out of gear and turn off the engine. I coast down the hill for about 100 metres until I am half way to the house where the drive begins to incline. I gasp for breath. I look down at my pants, my crotch is dark, but I can't see in the half light and can't work out if I have pissed myself or if it's the blood. I get out of the car slowly, my body is heavy and I walk towards the house. My shoes are full of blood, I try to walk again but I am falling from foot to foot, staggering, stumbling, everything is moving more slowly. The note inside *The Conscience of the Eye*, in the pocket of Aston's yellow mackintosh is tearing at my mind. I lie down; I struggle to breathe. I am no more than 20 metres from the beach. The sphere of the power station lurks above, stark in contrast to the sky. The long grass surrounds me, vibrant green, and then suddenly I see everything in black and

white, a French noir pastiche, I fall into cinematic vision, a monochromatic world, like Sterne's blue monster, its sad, ashamed head hung down, staring at its feet. My sight's getting dimmer. And my body's getting colder. And my mind's working slower. And I try to push my coat against the wound, but it starts to bleed again. And there is no one around. And as I lie there, camouflaged by the grass, I imagine her making her way from the house towards me. And it's then, and only then, that I realise what the question could have been. It would have been easier in fewer words.

Mary Aurory Sorry. We had thought they were Spencer's words in the days following what happened at the club. They weren't; Spencer had no sense of regret. He had seen it coming. I heard Murray's footsteps jogging up the stairs:

"I forgot the letter."
"It's on the draining board." I replied.
"Yeah, I know."

And he was gone. I envied him; he'd always known what he wanted. He was focused and seemed to fill every moment; well at least it looked that way to me. He was also probably the unluckiest person I had met, with his situation and all, but even through the worst of it he continually oozed with optimism.

I went back to the kitchen table, it was filled with Murray's clutter. I made space and then sat there for about ten minutes just staring at the pile of unopened mail and unread newspapers on top of the fridge. Murray wouldn't throw them out; he kept insisting he'd go through it all one day. It hadn't occurred to me before, but as I was looking at the pile I realised that he'd been keeping them since around the time she left. It seemed strange that he wouldn't open them; if she were going to contact any of us it was most likely that it would be him. I picked up a pen, but I was having trouble starting. I was stuck. I walked over to the sink and looked out of the window for a while. The snow wasn't falling anymore and the ploughs were out again. I could see their pulsing yellow lights bouncing off the buildings. I remembered her telling me about her father shifting snow; he also drove a plough. She had told me he was a man who loved the snow, and by all accounts a cold man. With the thaw came his obstacle; showing some type of affection to her. Everyone had their obstacle.

Earlier in the year, after Vivi had passed away and after they had finished the book, I thought it would all return to the way it was before. I thought the energy would come back, but it didn't. No sooner than Spencer had found the courage to return, Marie had gone. Abbé missed her the most. It was tragic seeing him walk around like that, always with a spray can in his bag. It started appearing in the autumn. At first only around the neighbourhood on boarded-up windows and derelict

property. Then as time passed, other places. On overpasses above the periphery and so on. That's when it started to become a bit like a fable, you'd sometimes hear people talking about it on the street. Stories began to circulate about who was responsible and the meaning of it. His efforts weren't stylised in any way. It looked just like big handwriting, executed without care. I saw him once from the kitchen window. You could see how familiar the formation of those letters in that particular order had become to him. It was almost automatic. He was lost in his own recursive narrative. It was devastating seeing him in the act. Taking the can from his bag, he didn't look around to see if anyone was watching him, he wrote it and walked away, passing on to another part of the city, another bus shelter or billboard. It had become his obstacle now. I went back and sat at the table, where the vase sat containing seeds of carnivorous plants that Aston had been collecting for a work. Seeds that consume. It was almost impossible to write. An hour or so later I put pen to paper. It began, 'Marie Aurore, forget about good. It's robbing us of our joy. It's robbing us with the sight of what we might have known. I once wrote a letter to Spencer not too dissimilar to this…' I can't remember it word for word, but something left me with each and every word that passed through that pen onto the page, I gradually unanchored myself from his weight. But it would have no effect on what was about to happen; the weight would still pull me down. I would die in the coming days, and my death would come slowly.

When the knife slips between my ribs, I initially think it's an accident, then after a few moments I realise it is intentional. Intentional, but perhaps a blunder? Mistaken identity. I don't see my assailant. It's crowded outside the bar, but everything is calm, no screams, no one even notices anything abnormal. I stumble away. I know I am wounded, but not fatally. I drop my weight back into the car seat, take the keys out of my coat pocket and slowly drive east. I light a cigarette as I queue for the slip road onto The Highway. It isn't until I reach Leiston that I realise how bad it is. As I approach the house it's dawn. I turn off the headlights on the car at the end of the drive, take it out of gear and turn off the engine. I coast down the hill for about 100 metres until I am half way to the house where the drive begins to incline. I gasp for breath. I look down at my pants, my crotch is dark, but I can't see in the half light and can't work out if I have pissed myself or if it's the blood. I get out of the car slowly, my body is heavy and I walk towards the house. My shoes are full of blood, I try to walk again but I am falling from foot to foot, staggering, stumbling, everything is moving more slowly. The note inside The Conscience of the Eye, in the pocket of Aston's yellow mackintosh is tearing at my mind. I lie down; I struggle to breathe. I am no more than 20 metres from the beach. The sphere of the power station lurks above, stark in contrast to the sky. The long grass surrounds me, vibrant green, and then suddenly I see everything in black and

white, a French noir pastiche, I fall into cinematic vision, a monochromatic world, like Sterne's blue monster, its sad, ashamed head hung down, staring at its feet. My sight's getting dimmer. And my body's getting colder. And my mind's working slower. And I try to push my coat against the wound, but it starts to bleed again. And there is no one around. And as I lie there, camouflaged by the grass, I imagine her making her way from the house towards me. And it's then, and only then, that I realise what the question could have been. It would have been easier in fewer words.

Mary Aurory Sorry. We had thought they were Spencer's words in the days following what happened at the club. They weren't; Spencer had no sense of regret. He had seen it coming. I heard Murray's footsteps jogging up the stairs:

"I forgot the letter."
"It's on the draining board." I replied.
"Yeah, I know."

And he was gone. I envied him; he'd always known what he wanted. He was focused and seemed to fill every moment; well at least it looked that way to me. He was also probably the unluckiest person I had met, with his situation and all, but even through the worst of it he continually oozed with optimism.

I went back to the kitchen table, it was filled with Murray's clutter. I made space and then sat there for about ten minutes just staring at the pile of unopened mail and unread newspapers on top of the fridge. Murray wouldn't throw them out; he kept insisting he'd go through it all one day. It hadn't occurred to me before, but as I was looking at the pile I realised that he'd been keeping them since around the time she left. It seemed strange that he wouldn't open them; if she were going to contact any of us it was most likely that it would be him. I picked up a pen, but I was having trouble starting. I was stuck. I walked over to the sink and looked out of the window for a while. The snow wasn't falling anymore and the ploughs were out again. I could see their pulsing yellow lights bouncing off the buildings. I remembered her telling me about her father shifting snow; he also drove a plough. She had told me he was a man who loved the snow, and by all accounts a cold man. With the thaw came his obstacle; showing some type of affection to her. Everyone had their obstacle.

Earlier in the year, after Vivi had passed away and after they had finished the book, I thought it would all return to the way it was before. I thought the energy would come back, but it didn't. No sooner than Spencer had found the courage to return, Marie had gone. Abbé missed her the most. It was tragic seeing him walk around like that, always with a spray can in his bag. It started appearing in the autumn. At first only around the neighbourhood on boarded-up windows and derelict

property. Then as time passed, other places. On overpasses above the periphery and so on. That's when it started to become a bit like a fable, you'd sometimes hear people talking about it on the street. Stories began to circulate about who was responsible and the meaning of it. His efforts weren't stylised in any way. It looked just like big handwriting, executed without care. I saw him once from the kitchen window. You could see how familiar the formation of those letters in that particular order had become to him. It was almost automatic. He was lost in his own recursive narrative. It was devastating seeing him in the act. Taking the can from his bag, he didn't look around to see if anyone was watching him, he wrote it and walked away, passing on to another part of the city, another bus shelter or billboard. It had become his obstacle now. I went back and sat at the table, where the vase sat containing seeds of carnivorous plants that Aston had been collecting for a work. Seeds that consume. It was almost impossible to write. An hour or so later I put pen to paper. It began, 'Marie Aurore, forget about good. It's robbing us of our joy. It's robbing us with the sight of what we might have known. I once wrote a letter to Spencer not too dissimilar to this...' I can't remember it word for word, but something left me with each and every word that passed through that pen onto the page, I gradually unanchored myself from his weight. But it would have no effect on what was about to happen; the weight would still pull me down. I would die in the coming days, and my death would come slowly.

When the knife slips between my ribs, I initially think it's an accident, then after a few moments I realise it is intentional. Intentional, but perhaps a blunder? Mistaken identity. I don't see my assailant. It's crowded outside the bar, but everything is calm, no screams, no one even notices anything abnormal. I stumble away. I know I am wounded, but not fatally. I drop my weight back into the car seat, take the keys out of my coat pocket and slowly drive east. I light a cigarette as I queue for the slip road onto The Highway. It isn't until I reach Leiston that I realise how bad it is. As I approach the house it's dawn. I turn off the headlights on the car at the end of the drive, take it out of gear and turn off the engine. I coast down the hill for about 100 metres until I am half way to the house where the drive begins to incline. I gasp for breath. I look down at my pants, my crotch is dark, but I can't see in the half light and can't work out if I have pissed myself or if it's the blood. I get out of the car slowly, my body is heavy and I walk towards the house. My shoes are full of blood, I try to walk again but I am falling from foot to foot, staggering, stumbling, everything is moving more slowly. The note inside The Conscience of the Eye, in the pocket of Aston's yellow mackintosh is tearing at my mind. I lie down; I struggle to breathe. I am no more than 20 metres from the beach. The sphere of the power station lurks above, stark in contrast to the sky. The long grass surrounds me, vibrant green, and then suddenly I see everything in black and

white, a French noir pastiche, I fall into cinematic vision, a monochromatic world, like Sterne's blue monster, its sad, ashamed head hung down, staring at its feet. My sight's getting dimmer. And my body's getting colder. And my mind's working slower. And I try to push my coat against the wound, but it starts to bleed again. And there is no one around. And as I lie there, camouflaged by the grass, I imagine her making her way from the house towards me. And it's then, and only then, that I realise what the question could have been. It would have been easier in fewer words.

Mary Aurory Sorry. We had thought they were Spencer's words in the days following what happened at the club. They weren't; Spencer had no sense of regret. He had seen it coming. I heard Murray's footsteps jogging up the stairs:

"I forgot the letter."
"It's on the draining board." I replied.
"Yeah, I know."

And he was gone. I envied him; he'd always known what he wanted. He was focused and seemed to fill every moment; well at least it looked that way to me. He was also probably the unluckiest person I had met, with his situation and all, but even through the worst of it he continually oozed with optimism.

I went back to the kitchen table, it was filled with Murray's clutter. I made space and then sat there for about ten minutes just staring at the pile of unopened mail and unread newspapers on top of the fridge. Murray wouldn't throw them out; he kept insisting he'd go through it all one day. It hadn't occurred to me before, but as I was looking at the pile I realised that he'd been keeping them since around the time she left. It seemed strange that he wouldn't open them; if she were going to contact any of us it was most likely that it would be him. I picked up a pen, but I was having trouble starting. I was stuck. I walked over to the sink and looked out of the window for a while. The snow wasn't falling anymore and the ploughs were out again. I could see their pulsing yellow lights bouncing off the buildings. I remembered her telling me about her father shifting snow; he also drove a plough. She had told me he was a man who loved the snow, and by all accounts a cold man. With the thaw came his obstacle; showing some type of affection to her. Everyone had their obstacle.

Earlier in the year, after Vivi had passed away and after they had finished the book, I thought it would all return to the way it was before. I thought the energy would come back, but it didn't. No sooner than Spencer had found the courage to return, Marie had gone. Abbé missed her the most. It was tragic seeing him walk around like that, always with a spray can in his bag. It started appearing in the autumn. At first only around the neighbourhood on boarded-up windows and derelict

property. Then as time passed, other places. On overpasses above the periphery and so on. That's when it started to become a bit like a fable, you'd sometimes hear people talking about it on the street. Stories began to circulate about who was responsible and the meaning of it. His efforts weren't stylised in any way. It looked just like big handwriting, executed without care. I saw him once from the kitchen window. You could see how familiar the formation of those letters in that particular order had become to him. It was almost automatic. He was lost in his own recursive narrative. It was devastating seeing him in the act. Taking the can from his bag, he didn't look around to see if anyone was watching him, he wrote it and walked away, passing on to another part of the city, another bus shelter or billboard. It had become his obstacle now. I went back and sat at the table, where the vase sat containing seeds of carnivorous plants that Aston had been collecting for a work. Seeds that consume. It was almost impossible to write. An hour or so later I put pen to paper. It began, 'Marie Aurore, forget about good. It's robbing us of our joy. It's robbing us with the sight of what we might have known. I once wrote a letter to Spencer not too dissimilar to this…' I can't remember it word for word, but something left me with each and every word that passed through that pen onto the page, I gradually unanchored myself from his weight. But it would have no effect on what was about to happen; the weight would still pull me down. I would die in the coming days, and my death would come slowly.

When the knife slips between my ribs, I initially think it's an accident, then after a few moments I realise it is intentional. Intentional, but perhaps a blunder? Mistaken identity. I don't see my assailant. It's crowded outside the bar, but everything is calm, no screams, no one even notices anything abnormal. I stumble away. I know I am wounded, but not fatally. I drop my weight back into the car seat, take the keys out of my coat pocket and slowly drive east. I light a cigarette as I queue for the slip road onto The Highway. It isn't until I reach Leiston that I realise how bad it is. As I approach the house it's dawn. I turn off the headlights on the car at the end of the drive, take it out of gear and turn off the engine. I coast down the hill for about 100 metres until I am half way to the house where the drive begins to incline. I gasp for breath. I look down at my pants, my crotch is dark, but I can't see in the half light and can't work out if I have pissed myself or if it's the blood. I get out of the car slowly, my body is heavy and I walk towards the house. My shoes are full of blood, I try to walk again but I am falling from foot to foot, staggering, stumbling, everything is moving more slowly. The note inside The Conscience of the Eye, in the pocket of Aston's yellow mackintosh is tearing at my mind. I lie down; I struggle to breathe. I am no more than 20 metres from the beach. The sphere of the power station lurks above, stark in contrast to the sky. The long grass surrounds me, vibrant green, and then suddenly I see everything in black and

white, a French noir pastiche, I fall into cinematic vision, a monochromatic world, like Sterne's blue monster, its sad, ashamed head hung down, staring at its feet. My sight's getting dimmer. And my body's getting colder. And my mind's working slower. And I try to push my coat against the wound, but it starts to bleed again. And there is no one around. And as I lie there, camouflaged by the grass, I imagine her making her way from the house towards me. And it's then, and only then, that I realise what the question could have been. It would have been easier in fewer words.

Mary Aurory Sorry. We had thought they were Spencer's words in the days following what happened at the club. They weren't; Spencer had no sense of regret. He had seen it coming. I heard Murray's footsteps jogging up the stairs:

"I forgot the letter."
"It's on the draining board." I replied.
"Yeah, I know."

And he was gone. I envied him; he'd always known what he wanted. He was focused and seemed to fill every moment; well at least it looked that way to me. He was also probably the unluckiest person I had met, with his situation and all, but even through the worst of it he continually oozed with optimism.

I went back to the kitchen table, it was filled with Murray's clutter. I made space and then sat there for about ten minutes just staring at the pile of unopened mail and unread newspapers on top of the fridge. Murray wouldn't throw them out; he kept insisting he'd go through it all one day. It hadn't occurred to me before, but as I was looking at the pile I realised that he'd been keeping them since around the time she left. It seemed strange that he wouldn't open them; if she were going to contact any of us it was most likely that it would be him. I picked up a pen, but I was having trouble starting. I was stuck. I walked over to the sink and looked out of the window for a while. The snow wasn't falling anymore and the ploughs were out again. I could see their pulsing yellow lights bouncing off the buildings. I remembered her telling me about her father shifting snow; he also drove a plough. She had told me he was a man who loved the snow, and by all accounts a cold man. With the thaw came his obstacle; showing some type of affection to her. Everyone had their obstacle.

Earlier in the year, after Vivi had passed away and after they had finished the book, I thought it would all return to the way it was before. I thought the energy would come back, but it didn't. No sooner than Spencer had found the courage to return, Marie had gone. Abbé missed her the most. It was tragic seeing him walk around like that, always with a spray can in his bag. It started appearing in the autumn. At first only around the neighbourhood on boarded-up windows and derelict

property. Then as time passed, other places. On overpasses above the periphery and so on. That's when it started to become a bit like a fable, you'd sometimes hear people talking about it on the street. Stories began to circulate about who was responsible and the meaning of it. His efforts weren't stylised in any way. It looked just like big handwriting, executed without care. I saw him once from the kitchen window. You could see how familiar the formation of those letters in that particular order had become to him. It was almost automatic. He was lost in his own recursive narrative. It was devastating seeing him in the act. Taking the can from his bag, he didn't look around to see if anyone was watching him, he wrote it and walked away, passing on to another part of the city, another bus shelter or billboard. It had become his obstacle now. I went back and sat at the table, where the vase sat containing seeds of carnivorous plants that Aston had been collecting for a work. Seeds that consume. It was almost impossible to write. An hour or so later I put pen to paper. It began, 'Marie Aurore, forget about good. It's robbing us of our joy. It's robbing us with the sight of what we might have known. I once wrote a letter to Spencer not too dissimilar to this…' I can't remember it word for word, but something left me with each and every word that passed through that pen onto the page, I gradually unanchored myself from his weight. But it would have no effect on what was about to happen; the weight would still pull me down. I would die in the coming days, and my death would come slowly.

When the knife slips between my ribs, I initially think it's an accident, then after a few moments I realise it is intentional. Intentional, but perhaps a blunder? Mistaken identity. I don't see my assailant. It's crowded outside the bar, but everything is calm, no screams, no one even notices anything abnormal. I stumble away. I know I am wounded, but not fatally. I drop my weight back into the car seat, take the keys out of my coat pocket and slowly drive east. I light a cigarette as I queue for the slip road onto The Highway. It isn't until I reach Leiston that I realise how bad it is. As I approach the house it's dawn. I turn off the headlights on the car at the end of the drive, take it out of gear and turn off the engine. I coast down the hill for about 100 metres until I am half way to the house where the drive begins to incline. I gasp for breath. I look down at my pants, my crotch is dark, but I can't see in the half light and can't work out if I have pissed myself or if it's the blood. I get out of the car slowly, my body is heavy and I walk towards the house. My shoes are full of blood, I try to walk again but I am falling from foot to foot, staggering, stumbling, everything is moving more slowly. The note inside The Conscience of the Eye, in the pocket of Aston's yellow mackintosh is tearing at my mind. I lie down; I struggle to breathe. I am no more than 20 metres from the beach. The sphere of the power station lurks above, stark in contrast to the sky. The long grass surrounds me, vibrant green, and then suddenly I see everything in black and

white, a French noir pastiche, I fall into cinematic vision, a monochromatic world, like Sterne's blue monster, its sad, ashamed head hung down, staring at its feet. My sight's getting dimmer. And my body's getting colder. And my mind's working slower. And I try to push my coat against the wound, but it starts to bleed again. And there is no one around. And as I lie there, camouflaged by the grass, I imagine her making her way from the house towards me. And it's then, and only then, that I realise what the question could have been. It would have been easier in fewer words.

Mary Aurory Sorry. We had thought they were Spencer's words in the days following what happened at the club. They weren't; Spencer had no sense of regret. He had seen it coming. I heard Murray's footsteps jogging up the stairs:

"I forgot the letter."
"It's on the draining board." I replied.
"Yeah, I know."

And he was gone. I envied him; he'd always known what he wanted. He was focused and seemed to fill every moment; well at least it looked that way to me. He was also probably the unluckiest person I had met, with his situation and all, but even through the worst of it he continually oozed with optimism.

I went back to the kitchen table, it was filled with Murray's clutter. I made space and then sat there for about ten minutes just staring at the pile of unopened mail and unread newspapers on top of the fridge. Murray wouldn't throw them out; he kept insisting he'd go through it all one day. It hadn't occurred to me before, but as I was looking at the pile I realised that he'd been keeping them since around the time she left. It seemed strange that he wouldn't open them; if she were going to contact any of us it was most likely that it would be him. I picked up a pen, but I was having trouble starting. I was stuck. I walked over to the sink and looked out of the window for a while. The snow wasn't falling anymore and the ploughs were out again. I could see their pulsing yellow lights bouncing off the buildings. I remembered her telling me about her father shifting snow; he also drove a plough. She had told me he was a man who loved the snow, and by all accounts a cold man. With the thaw came his obstacle; showing some type of affection to her. Everyone had their obstacle.

Earlier in the year, after Vivi had passed away and after they had finished the book, I thought it would all return to the way it was before. I thought the energy would come back, but it didn't. No sooner than Spencer had found the courage to return, Marie had gone. Abbé missed her the most. It was tragic seeing him walk around like that, always with a spray can in his bag. It started appearing in the autumn. At first only around the neighbourhood on boarded-up windows and derelict

property. Then as time passed, other places. On overpasses above the periphery and so on. That's when it started to become a bit like a fable, you'd sometimes hear people talking about it on the street. Stories began to circulate about who was responsible and the meaning of it. His efforts weren't stylised in any way. It looked just like big handwriting, executed without care. I saw him once from the kitchen window. You could see how familiar the formation of those letters in that particular order had become to him. It was almost automatic. He was lost in his own recursive narrative. It was devastating seeing him in the act. Taking the can from his bag, he didn't look around to see if anyone was watching him, he wrote it and walked away, passing on to another part of the city, another bus shelter or billboard. It had become his obstacle now. I went back and sat at the table, where the vase sat containing seeds of carnivorous plants that Aston had been collecting for a work. Seeds that consume. It was almost impossible to write. An hour or so later I put pen to paper. It began, 'Marie Aurore, forget about good. It's robbing us of our joy. It's robbing us with the sight of what we might have known. I once wrote a letter to Spencer not too dissimilar to this...' I can't remember it word for word, but something left me with each and every word that passed through that pen onto the page, I gradually unanchored myself from his weight. But it would have no effect on what was about to happen; the weight would still pull me down. I would die in the coming days, and my death would come slowly.

When the knife slips between my ribs, I initially think it's an accident, then after a few moments I realise it is intentional. Intentional, but perhaps a blunder? Mistaken identity. I don't see my assailant. It's crowded outside the bar, but everything is calm, no screams, no one even notices anything abnormal. I stumble away. I know I am wounded, but not fatally. I drop my weight back into the car seat, take the keys out of my coat pocket and slowly drive east. I light a cigarette as I queue for the slip road onto The Highway. It isn't until I reach Leiston that I realise how bad it is. As I approach the house it's dawn. I turn off the headlights on the car at the end of the drive, take it out of gear and turn off the engine. I coast down the hill for about 100 metres until I am half way to the house where the drive begins to incline. I gasp for breath. I look down at my pants, my crotch is dark, but I can't see in the half light and can't work out if I have pissed myself or if it's the blood. I get out of the car slowly, my body is heavy and I walk towards the house. My shoes are full of blood, I try to walk again but I am falling from foot to foot, staggering, stumbling, everything is moving more slowly. The note inside The Conscience of the Eye, in the pocket of Aston's yellow mackintosh is tearing at my mind. I lie down; I struggle to breathe. I am no more than 20 metres from the beach. The sphere of the power station lurks above, stark in contrast to the sky. The long grass surrounds me, vibrant green, and then suddenly I see everything in black and

white, a French noir pastiche, I fall into cinematic vision, a monochromatic world, like Sterne's blue monster, its sad, ashamed head hung down, staring at its feet. My sight's getting dimmer. And my body's getting colder. And my mind's working slower. And I try to push my coat against the wound, but it starts to bleed again. And there is no one around. And as I lie there, camouflaged by the grass, I imagine her making her way from the house towards me. And it's then, and only then, that I realise what the question could have been. It would have been easier in fewer words.

Mary Aurory Sorry. We had thought they were Spencer's words in the days following what happened at the club. They weren't; Spencer had no sense of regret. He had seen it coming. I heard Murray's footsteps jogging up the stairs:

"I forgot the letter."
"It's on the draining board." I replied.
"Yeah, I know."

And he was gone. I envied him; he'd always known what he wanted. He was focused and seemed to fill every moment; well at least it looked that way to me. He was also probably the unluckiest person I had met, with his situation and all, but even through the worst of it he continually oozed with optimism.

I went back to the kitchen table, it was filled with Murray's clutter. I made space and then sat there for about ten minutes just staring at the pile of unopened mail and unread newspapers on top of the fridge. Murray wouldn't throw them out; he kept insisting he'd go through it all one day. It hadn't occurred to me before, but as I was looking at the pile I realised that he'd been keeping them since around the time she left. It seemed strange that he wouldn't open them; if she were going to contact any of us it was most likely that it would be him. I picked up a pen, but I was having trouble starting. I was stuck. I walked over to the sink and looked out of the window for a while. The snow wasn't falling anymore and the ploughs were out again. I could see their pulsing yellow lights bouncing off the buildings. I remembered her telling me about her father shifting snow; he also drove a plough. She had told me he was a man who loved the snow, and by all accounts a cold man. With the thaw came his obstacle; showing some type of affection to her. Everyone had their obstacle.

Earlier in the year, after Vivi had passed away and after they had finished the book, I thought it would all return to the way it was before. I thought the energy would come back, but it didn't. No sooner than Spencer had found the courage to return, Marie had gone. Abbé missed her the most. It was tragic seeing him walk around like that, always with a spray can in his bag. It started appearing in the autumn. At first only around the neighbourhood on boarded-up windows and derelict

property. Then as time passed, other places. On overpasses above the periphery and so on. That's when it started to become a bit like a fable, you'd sometimes hear people talking about it on the street. Stories began to circulate about who was responsible and the meaning of it. His efforts weren't stylised in any way. It looked just like big handwriting, executed without care. I saw him once from the kitchen window. You could see how familiar the formation of those letters in that particular order had become to him. It was almost automatic. He was lost in his own recursive narrative. It was devastating seeing him in the act. Taking the can from his bag, he didn't look around to see if anyone was watching him, he wrote it and walked away, passing on to another part of the city, another bus shelter or billboard. It had become his obstacle now. I went back and sat at the table, where the vase sat containing seeds of carnivorous plants that Aston had been collecting for a work. Seeds that consume. It was almost impossible to write. An hour or so later I put pen to paper. It began, 'Marie Aurore, forget about good. It's robbing us of our joy. It's robbing us with the sight of what we might have known. I once wrote a letter to Spencer not too dissimilar to this...' I can't remember it word for word, but something left me with each and every word that passed through that pen onto the page, I gradually unanchored myself from his weight. But it would have no effect on what was about to happen; the weight would still pull me down. I would die in the coming days, and my death would come slowly.

When the knife slips between my ribs, I initially think it's an accident, then after a few moments I realise it is intentional. Intentional, but perhaps a blunder? Mistaken identity. I don't see my assailant. It's crowded outside the bar, but everything is calm, no screams, no one even notices anything abnormal. I stumble away. I know I am wounded, but not fatally. I drop my weight back into the car seat, take the keys out of my coat pocket and slowly drive east. I light a cigarette as I queue for the slip road onto The Highway. It isn't until I reach Leiston that I realise how bad it is. As I approach the house it's dawn. I turn off the headlights on the car at the end of the drive, take it out of gear and turn off the engine. I coast down the hill for about 100 metres until I am half way to the house where the drive begins to incline. I gasp for breath. I look down at my pants, my crotch is dark, but I can't see in the half light and can't work out if I have pissed myself or if it's the blood. I get out of the car slowly, my body is heavy and I walk towards the house. My shoes are full of blood, I try to walk again but I am falling from foot to foot, staggering, stumbling, everything is moving more slowly. The note inside The Conscience of the Eye, in the pocket of Aston's yellow mackintosh is tearing at my mind. I lie down; I struggle to breathe. I am no more than 20 metres from the beach. The sphere of the power station lurks above, stark in contrast to the sky. The long grass surrounds me, vibrant green, and then suddenly I see everything in black and

white, a French noir pastiche, I fall into cinematic vision, a monochromatic world, like Sterne's blue monster, its sad, ashamed head hung down, staring at its feet. My sight's getting dimmer. And my body's getting colder. And my mind's working slower. And I try to push my coat against the wound, but it starts to bleed again. And there is no one around. And as I lie there, camouflaged by the grass, I imagine her making her way from the house towards me. And it's then, and only then, that I realise what the question could have been. It would have been easier in fewer words.

Mary Aurory Sorry. We had thought they were Spencer's words in the days following what happened at the club. They weren't; Spencer had no sense of regret. He had seen it coming. I heard Murray's footsteps jogging up the stairs:

"I forgot the letter."
"It's on the draining board." I replied.
"Yeah, I know."

And he was gone. I envied him; he'd always known what he wanted. He was focused and seemed to fill every moment; well at least it looked that way to me. He was also probably the unluckiest person I had met, with his situation and all, but even through the worst of it he continually oozed with optimism.

I went back to the kitchen table, it was filled with Murray's clutter. I made space and then sat there for about ten minutes just staring at the pile of unopened mail and unread newspapers on top of the fridge. Murray wouldn't throw them out; he kept insisting he'd go through it all one day. It hadn't occurred to me before, but as I was looking at the pile I realised that he'd been keeping them since around the time she left. It seemed strange that he wouldn't open them; if she were going to contact any of us it was most likely that it would be him. I picked up a pen, but I was having trouble starting. I was stuck. I walked over to the sink and looked out of the window for a while. The snow wasn't falling anymore and the ploughs were out again. I could see their pulsing yellow lights bouncing off the buildings. I remembered her telling me about her father shifting snow; he also drove a plough. She had told me he was a man who loved the snow, and by all accounts a cold man. With the thaw came his obstacle; showing some type of affection to her. Everyone had their obstacle.

Earlier in the year, after Vivi had passed away and after they had finished the book, I thought it would all return to the way it was before. I thought the energy would come back, but it didn't. No sooner than Spencer had found the courage to return, Marie had gone. Abbé missed her the most. It was tragic seeing him walk around like that, always with a spray can in his bag. It started appearing in the autumn. At first only around the neighbourhood on boarded-up windows and derelict

property. Then as time passed, other places. On overpasses above the periphery and so on. That's when it started to become a bit like a fable, you'd sometimes hear people talking about it on the street. Stories began to circulate about who was responsible and the meaning of it. His efforts weren't stylised in any way. It looked just like big handwriting, executed without care. I saw him once from the kitchen window. You could see how familiar the formation of those letters in that particular order had become to him. It was almost automatic. He was lost in his own recursive narrative. It was devastating seeing him in the act. Taking the can from his bag, he didn't look around to see if anyone was watching him, he wrote it and walked away, passing on to another part of the city, another bus shelter or billboard. It had become his obstacle now. I went back and sat at the table, where the vase sat containing seeds of carnivorous plants that Aston had been collecting for a work. Seeds that consume. It was almost impossible to write. An hour or so later I put pen to paper. It began, 'Marie Aurore, forget about good. It's robbing us of our joy. It's robbing us with the sight of what we might have known. I once wrote a letter to Spencer not too dissimilar to this…' I can't remember it word for word, but something left me with each and every word that passed through that pen onto the page, I gradually unanchored myself from his weight. But it would have no effect on what was about to happen; the weight would still pull me down. I would die in the coming days, and my death would come slowly.

When the knife slips between my ribs, I initially think it's an accident, then after a few moments I realise it is intentional. Intentional, but perhaps a blunder? Mistaken identity. I don't see my assailant. It's crowded outside the bar, but everything is calm, no screams, no one even notices anything abnormal. I stumble away. I know I am wounded, but not fatally. I drop my weight back into the car seat, take the keys out of my coat pocket and slowly drive east. I light a cigarette as I queue for the slip road onto The Highway. It isn't until I reach Leiston that I realise how bad it is. As I approach the house it's dawn. I turn off the headlights on the car at the end of the drive, take it out of gear and turn off the engine. I coast down the hill for about 100 metres until I am half way to the house where the drive begins to incline. I gasp for breath. I look down at my pants, my crotch is dark, but I can't see in the half light and can't work out if I have pissed myself or if it's the blood. I get out of the car slowly, my body is heavy and I walk towards the house. My shoes are full of blood, I try to walk again but I am falling from foot to foot, staggering, stumbling, everything is moving more slowly. The note inside The Conscience of the Eye, in the pocket of Aston's yellow mackintosh is tearing at my mind. I lie down; I struggle to breathe. I am no more than 20 metres from the beach. The sphere of the power station lurks above, stark in contrast to the sky. The long grass surrounds me, vibrant green, and then suddenly I see everything in black and

white, a French noir pastiche, I fall into cinematic vision, a monochromatic world, like Sterne's blue monster, its sad, ashamed head hung down, staring at its feet. My sight's getting dimmer. And my body's getting colder. And my mind's working slower. And I try to push my coat against the wound, but it starts to bleed again. And there is no one around. And as I lie there, camouflaged by the grass, I imagine her making her way from the house towards me. And it's then, and only then, that I realise what the question could have been. It would have been easier in fewer words.

Mary Aurory Sorry. We had thought they were Spencer's words in the days following what happened at the club. They weren't; Spencer had no sense of regret. He had seen it coming. I heard Murray's footsteps jogging up the stairs:

"I forgot the letter."
"It's on the draining board." I replied.
"Yeah, I know."

And he was gone. I envied him; he'd always known what he wanted. He was focused and seemed to fill every moment; well at least it looked that way to me. He was also probably the unluckiest person I had met, with his situation and all, but even through the worst of it he continually oozed with optimism.

I went back to the kitchen table, it was filled with Murray's clutter. I made space and then sat there for about ten minutes just staring at the pile of unopened mail and unread newspapers on top of the fridge. Murray wouldn't throw them out; he kept insisting he'd go through it all one day. It hadn't occurred to me before, but as I was looking at the pile I realised that he'd been keeping them since around the time she left. It seemed strange that he wouldn't open them; if she were going to contact any of us it was most likely that it would be him. I picked up a pen, but I was having trouble starting. I was stuck. I walked over to the sink and looked out of the window for a while. The snow wasn't falling anymore and the ploughs were out again. I could see their pulsing yellow lights bouncing off the buildings. I remembered her telling me about her father shifting snow; he also drove a plough. She had told me he was a man who loved the snow, and by all accounts a cold man. With the thaw came his obstacle; showing some type of affection to her. Everyone had their obstacle.

Earlier in the year, after Vivi had passed away and after they had finished the book, I thought it would all return to the way it was before. I thought the energy would come back, but it didn't. No sooner than Spencer had found the courage to return, Marie had gone. Abbé missed her the most. It was tragic seeing him walk around like that, always with a spray can in his bag. It started appearing in the autumn. At first only around the neighbourhood on boarded-up windows and derelict

property. Then as time passed, other places. On overpasses above the periphery and so on. That's when it started to become a bit like a fable, you'd sometimes hear people talking about it on the street. Stories began to circulate about who was responsible and the meaning of it. His efforts weren't stylised in any way. It looked just like big handwriting, executed without care. I saw him once from the kitchen window. You could see how familiar the formation of those letters in that particular order had become to him. It was almost automatic. He was lost in his own recursive narrative. It was devastating seeing him in the act. Taking the can from his bag, he didn't look around to see if anyone was watching him, he wrote it and walked away, passing on to another part of the city, another bus shelter or billboard. It had become his obstacle now. I went back and sat at the table, where the vase sat containing seeds of carnivorous plants that Aston had been collecting for a work. Seeds that consume. It was almost impossible to write. An hour or so later I put pen to paper. It began, 'Marie Aurore, forget about good. It's robbing us of our joy. It's robbing us with the sight of what we might have known. I once wrote a letter to Spencer not too dissimilar to this…' I can't remember it word for word, but something left me with each and every word that passed through that pen onto the page, I gradually unanchored myself from his weight. But it would have no effect on what was about to happen; the weight would still pull me down. I would die in the coming days, and my death would come slowly.

When the knife slips between my ribs, I initially think it's an accident, then after a few moments I realise it is intentional. Intentional, but perhaps a blunder? Mistaken identity. I don't see my assailant. It's crowded outside the bar, but everything is calm, no screams, no one even notices anything abnormal. I stumble away. I know I am wounded, but not fatally. I drop my weight back into the car seat, take the keys out of my coat pocket and slowly drive east. I light a cigarette as I queue for the slip road onto The Highway. It isn't until I reach Leiston that I realise how bad it is. As I approach the house it's dawn. I turn off the headlights on the car at the end of the drive, take it out of gear and turn off the engine. I coast down the hill for about 100 metres until I am half way to the house where the drive begins to incline. I gasp for breath. I look down at my pants, my crotch is dark, but I can't see in the half light and can't work out if I have pissed myself or if it's the blood. I get out of the car slowly, my body is heavy and I walk towards the house. My shoes are full of blood, I try to walk again but I am falling from foot to foot, staggering, stumbling, everything is moving more slowly. The note inside The Conscience of the Eye, in the pocket of Aston's yellow mackintosh is tearing at my mind. I lie down; I struggle to breathe. I am no more than 20 metres from the beach. The sphere of the power station lurks above, stark in contrast to the sky. The long grass surrounds me, vibrant green, and then suddenly I see everything in black and

white, a French noir pastiche, I fall into cinematic vision, a monochromatic world, like Sterne's blue monster, its sad, ashamed head hung down, staring at its feet. My sight's getting dimmer. And my body's getting colder. And my mind's working slower. And I try to push my coat against the wound, but it starts to bleed again. And there is no one around. And as I lie there, camouflaged by the grass, I imagine her making her way from the house towards me. And it's then, and only then, that I realise what the question could have been. It would have been easier in fewer words.

Mary Aurory Sorry. We had thought they were Spencer's words in the days following what happened at the club. They weren't; Spencer had no sense of regret. He had seen it coming. I heard Murray's footsteps jogging up the stairs.

"I forgot the letter."
"It's on the draining board." I replied.
"Yeah, I know."

And he was gone. I envied him; he'd always known what he wanted. He was focused and seemed to fill every moment; well at least it looked that way to me. He was also probably the unluckiest person I had met, with his situation and all, but even through the worst of it he continually oozed with optimism.

I went back to the kitchen table, it was filled with Murray's clutter. I made space and then sat there for about ten minutes just staring at the pile of unopened mail and unread newspapers on top of the fridge. Murray wouldn't throw them out; he kept insisting he'd go through it all one day. It hadn't occurred to me before, but as I was looking at the pile I realised that he'd been keeping them since around the time she left. It seemed strange that he wouldn't open them; if she were going to contact any of us it was most likely that it would be him. I picked up a pen, but I was having trouble starting. I was stuck. I walked over to the sink and looked out of the window for a while. The snow wasn't falling anymore and the ploughs were out again. I could see their pulsing yellow lights bouncing off the buildings. I remembered her telling me about her father shifting snow; he also drove a plough. She had told me he was a man who loved the snow, and by all accounts a cold man. With the thaw came his obstacle; showing some type of affection to her. Everyone had their obstacle.

Earlier in the year, after Vivi had passed away and after they had finished the book, I thought it would all return to the way it was before. I thought the energy would come back, but it didn't. No sooner than Spencer had found the courage to return, Marie had gone. Abbé missed her the most. It was tragic seeing him walk around like that, always with a spray can in his bag. It started appearing in the autumn. At first only around the neighbourhood on boarded-up windows and derelict

property. Then as time passed, other places. On overpasses above the periphery and so on. That's when it started to become a bit like a fable, you'd sometimes hear people talking about it on the street. Stories began to circulate about who was responsible and the meaning of it. His efforts weren't stylised in any way. It looked just like big handwriting, executed without care. I saw him once from the kitchen window. You could see how familiar the formation of those letters in that particular order had become to him. It was almost automatic. He was lost in his own recursive narrative. It was devastating seeing him in the act. Taking the can from his bag, he didn't look around to see if anyone was watching him, he wrote it and walked away, passing on to another part of the city, another bus shelter or billboard. It had become his obstacle now. I went back and sat at the table, where the vase sat containing seeds of carnivorous plants that Aston had been collecting for a work. Seeds that consume. It was almost impossible to write. An hour or so later I put pen to paper. It began, 'Marie Aurore, forget about good. It's robbing us of our joy. It's robbing us with the sight of what we might have known. I once wrote a letter to Spencer not too dissimilar to this...' I can't remember it word for word, but something left me with each and every word that passed through that pen onto the page, I gradually unanchored myself from his weight. But it would have no effect on what was about to happen; the weight would still pull me down. I would die in the coming days, and my death would come slowly.

PEGBOARD

A display-rack produced from pegboard and display wires representing all the books currently on the artist's desk.

In my house I have a lot of books, the majority of which I have not read (or rather have not finished), yet constantly I buy new books. I am very bad at finishing things, starting them is no trouble at all, but completion is a challenge. My problem of being easily distracted raises its head in most areas of my life, professionally and otherwise. In the kitchen, Spaghetti Bolognese becomes Chili con Carne within a matter of minutes; a visit to the bank can turn into a day trip to the Ideal Home Show; the self-assembly furniture in my daughter's bedroom lies partially assembled; and to the annoyance of my friends, conversations jump sporadically without conclusions nor apparent associations. I have to grit my teeth, clench my fists and force myself to finish whatever it is I have started. This does have its benefits though, as most of the logic in my practice, and the research at the heart of my investigations, is based on loose-associative methodology.[1]

Perhaps the area where my inability to complete things invades my life the most is in reading. For the majority of the books I own I have only read the first chapter (or at least the index page). You can tell an uncanny amount from beginnings, and as

1. It's human nature to associate, to draw connections. No matter how distant or disparate the relationship between two images, articles, objects or ideas, the ability to identify shared characteristics or affiliations will always exist. It may be true to say that it is more of a challenge not to find a connection between any two given articles than it is to find a

they are the parts that I enjoy the most, it makes sense that I should only give them time. Similarly, I find it difficult to finish writing texts. This text, for example, has started with the notion that I own more books than I have read, but unless I fight the urge and aim to remain understandable it may yet end on Chinese wok cooking, or Formula One car racing, or the uniform of a McDonald's drive-thru attendant. It's a struggle. This makes me wonder if I should only write in footnotes; an endless stream of sideline arguments and stories, references in references, shooting off at mad tangents, losing myself and illogically stuttering and mumbling (although I think Flann O'Brien already did this[2]).

A good friend of mine, Maki Suzuki, used to arrange the library in his living room in a very unique way. Open bookshelves were placed in the centre of his living room, so that he could get to both the front and the back. All the books he had read were placed with their spines pointing one way, all the books he hadn't read had their spines pointing the other. Ingenious. If you are writing a text and you are looking for a quote or a reference you go to one side of the shelf. If you are looking for a new book to read that you've not yet started you go to the other side. An unsurprisingly brilliant idea as it comes from a surprisingly brilliant mind. It would suit my inability to read a book from start to finish, only on the verso side I would show the

connection; irrespective of their history, heritage or place in the world, or how improvised or random their selection. The neurocognitive recognition of association has allowed for entire schools of thinking and research methodologies to evolve around the idea of the 'Loose Association', from 'Knight's Move Thinking' to Warburg Institute, London. The practice of linking a multitude of seemingly disparate and unrelated ideas has been put forward as a valid and interesting conduct of research and practice. When two articles are placed on a page or within a defined area, a framed border for example, the viewer is subliminally directed to search out and draw links. So what happens when the links are multiplied and the viewer is uncertain about whether they are acknowledging the right link? We are presented with a conundrum, something like a spot-the-difference between two identical images. A murder mystery puzzle with no murderer. A jigsaw without an image and pieces with the same interlocking pattern on each edge. We are presented with something that is intrinsically interesting, because with the utmost possible audacity it suggests the human brain is defunct; not being able to lock onto a common ground, leaving us crippled with a sort of spines of the books, not that I hadn't started, but books I hadn't finished. Perhaps embarrassing me into a forced completion. Like a satisfying to-do list; instead of crossing out items I could place a book back on the shelf with its spine facing the other way.

As it is I have two big tables either side of my desk at home, piled with a multitude of books, catalogues, comics, novels and periodicals – the knowledge contained within is essential to the development of the projects I have on. The trestles are buckling under the weight. The ones that I get bored of reading, or simply cannot muster the enthusiasm to finish, get put on the top of a series of piles on the floor, and the newer books, that never seem to stop arriving, take pride of place on the desk. The ones of any real urgency or importance, in this hierarchy of placement in my studio, are the ones on my desk. Their placement screams "READ ME" because I have positioned them so that it is almost impossible to reach my computer keyboard without first laying my hands on them. If I don't read these books, that are intentionally placed to get in my way, I might as well give up.

As I write this text, obstructing my keyboard is a catalogue of book display devices from an Italian manufacturer. It's here because I'm meant to be thinking and writing about the ingenious design of pegboard,[3] instead of rambling on. I could

neuro-cognitive feedback whining in our ears.

2. *The Third Policeman* (1967) by Flann O'Brien contains a weird sense of proportionality in every sense of the term's usage, (I always thought Will Self's *Scale* (1995) was absolute genius until I was introduced to *The Third Policeman*). This toying with the ability to interpret scale on a multitude of levels is even mirrored physically in the use of footnotes: as the book progresses, the footnotes get longer and the main body of text shorter.

3. Pegboard is tempered hardboard that is pre-drilled with evenly spaced holes. The holes are used to accept pegs or hooks to support various items, such as tools in a workshop.

now begin writing about why pegboard is brilliant, which would primarily be due to its adaptability. But for me pegboard is brilliant because of its nostalgia; it belongs in a world of derelict Milanese shop window displays, the ones viewed through a yellow window film to prevent sun-bleaching of the books on display, which have most likely been there for decades, longing to be started, never mind completed. I leaf through the catalogue and choose a sheet of pegboard large enough to fill the wall behind my computer monitor, above my desk and order enough wire frame display devices to place the small pile of "must read extremely urgently" books and catalogues situated around my keyboard. Space at last. A tidy studio is a tidy mind.

SMOKED VODKA

A bottle, partially buried in sand, containing smoked vodka produced by the artist.

For years now I've had an amateur interest in the creation of cocktails – the pretentious but correct terminology for this activity being 'mixology'. Making cocktails is easy, but mixology is entirely different. I'm interested in the similarities between the production of art and the invention of cocktails: the bringing together of ingredients (with all of the back-stories, histories and moments of cultural significance they hold), playing with or against one another, colliding well and colliding badly, and producing taste sensations and associations in the mind, which until then have not existed. My most successful cocktail, also an artwork (never one to miss a trick) entitled 'A Thinking Hand's Bequest' (2012)[1] was formed from sampling numerous cocktails and encounters in different cities across Japan, merging them into a drink that, for me, is as complex as Japanese culture and my presence within it.

My most unsuccessful idea for a cocktail that I have been tampering with over the last 18 months includes smoked vodka. Smoking is a boy scout activity I do in my garden at my home in the countryside, with a variety of things such as garlic, olive oil, salt, cheese and eggs. The idea of smoking vodka came to me one evening when I tasted some

1. 'A Thinking Hands Bequest' (2012)
- A single ice rock (measuring about 6 cm across)
- One shot of Shiso Plum Liqueur
- One shot of Edmond Briottet Liqueur de Violette
- Moët & Chandon Brut Imperial Champagne to top
- A single fresh black cherry (on steel cocktail sword)
- A star punched from lemon peel (no pith)

Served in a Martini glass for ladies and in a titanium or copper Moscow Mule mug for gentlemen. Pour Liqueurs slowly over the ice rock so that they remain separated, fill to top with champagne poured slowly over the

olive oil I had just smoked. As I lifted the jar to my mouth I inhaled the peaty odour, which made me cough and splutter as if the taste of oil and inhalation of the smoky vapour were the same thing. I thought it would transfer to smoked vodka perfectly. There is a long history of whisky distilled in burnt smoking barrels and there are cocktails incorporating chemicals that emit plumes of smoke from the glass, but to my knowledge there is no smoked cocktail. The problem is that although the idea of drinking a cocktail with the odour of smoke is a good one, the taste is inexorably revolting. In my quest to refine a recipe for a pleasant, drinkable smoked cocktail I have used many litres of alcohol and spent many hours at my smoker. All I had to show for it was a series of half-full jars of alcohol, smoked to varying degrees, in a full range of yellowy-brown hues, most with a fair amount of sediment settling within. It was difficult to know what to do with them as disposing of them seemed wrong after so much time and energy went into their production. Reminded of the song by The Police, 'Message in a Bottle', an idea occurred to me to take them to a nearby beach and drop them into the North Sea, hoping they would be washed up somewhere else, to be discovered by someone who would put them to more successful use. As car polish perhaps?

back of spoon so that three colour stratum are visible. Add a whole single black cherry to a cocktail sword and a small star of lemon peel.

Derived from a mingling of three encounters in tiny bars in Japan, 'A Thinking Hand's Bequest' (2012) is a variation on, or the association of: an Antique Gold from the Prince Park Tower skyline bar, Tokyo; an Ume-Shu liqueur spritzer with shiso leaf, of which Hoshiko is by far the best, produced by Danny Aikawa at a bar called Howl, Tokyo; and a Violet Lady, invented in 1959, by an elderly gentleman named Nishikawa at Bar Nishikawa Tei, Fukuoka. All of the flavours in these three cocktails remind me of being sleepless late at night in strange places with an appetite for more, in every sense. It's hard to explain the taste, although my 15 year-old sister-in-law told me it tastes just like a blue WKD.

AN AMAZON BOX

A standard cardboard box which previously delivered goods purchased on Amazon.co.uk, containing personal ephemera such as a household Yucca plant, a sports trophy, an assortment of folders, books, periodicals and a coffee mug.

Amazon's corporate pictographic logo – the smile which doubles as an arrow portraying the speed and efficiency of the delivery – is so intertwined with the typography of the word 'Amazon' that on the occasions that I have encountered the pictogram alone it has been impossible, in fact, to identify the company it represents. This often happens with the recognition of visual identity. If you were to see the 'B' from *Buffy the Vampire Slayer*, or the 'M' from Marriott Hotels without the wording, would you be able to identify them?

Last year I found a picture of the Amazon logo on a box in the background of an image of Steve Jobs at his home in Palo Alto, California, USA.[1] The image puzzled me and I had to email it to friends to ask for help identifying the logo. One replied: "Amazon, idiot!" This logo I had seen hundreds of times, I could not identify without the word. The book on Jobs described him being fired from Apple Inc. at the age of 30, a seemingly very public failure. There was a moment as I looked at the picture of him, that an image appeared in my head of him walking out of Apple Inc. with a few per-

1. Which incidentally is where the first Whole Foods Market was opened, the very store where I once saw two bearded women carrying yoga mats, dancing to Fleetwood Mac, which was playing over the Tannoy.

sonal possessions from his office, perhaps a family photo, a few folders, some books, a football trophy and a Yucca plant, housed in a cardboard Amazon box. One that had been accidently opened upside down, meaning its smile had been re-rendered as a sad mouth, down turned at its edges. Of course Amazon didn't exist when Steve Jobs was 30, but no need to spoil my imagination with fact.

HENRY

A well-used HVR200A vacuum cleaner produced by Numatic International Ltd, more commonly known as Henry.

.too good quite looks it And .it like I but ,fad a was it thought I beginning the In .air of amount greater a moves and store to easy ,clean to easy ,silent ,efficient power more ,economical ,simple it's ,fan bladed regular a to Compared .any t'aren there as blades the in fingers their stick can't they because kids have you if Especially .good quite actually it's is thing annoying The .'Multiplier Air' an ,fan Dyson a purchased recently I've

?go to meant water this is Where

.aperture Airblade the below casing large the into leaking perhaps or ,dryer hand the of side the down dribbling perhaps ,toilet the of humidity the into evaporating perhaps ,sits it there and bottom the at meet plastic of pieces two where crevasse a in collects hands your from pushed is that water the ;market the on dryer hand unhygienic most the is and electricity of amount vast a uses also It .market the on dryers hand noisiest the of one is it ,use singular a from suffer Airblade the does only Not .)emergencies rain and stain after clothes dry to ability its count you if fourth a and(use third and second a tool the giving ;hair the or face the into directed is airstream the that so down upside turned be can hands your to down air the directs that nozzle the that is dryer hand standard the of design ingenious The .bathroom public a in face my washed have I times Countless .does it all that's but ,replacing is it object the than faster seconds several user its of hands the dry does Airblade The .Enterprise Starship the off broken has that some-thing like looks it ;predecessor its as looking good as not is It .replacing is it tool the than larger times four is Dyson the Physically .Inc ,Dryer American by produced those to style in similar more dryers hand replaces Airblade Dyson The

[3].occasion the to rises imagination our only if skills our expand can ,too ,it ;possibilities unfathomed of manner all admits tool purpose-all this variety sheer its in But .screw as well as line and ,lift ,gouge can it since ,tool a such being to close comes screwdriver edged flat the ,cabinet maker's piano a In .case special a seems tool purpose-all The

.198 .p ,2008 ,Penguin ,*Craftsman The* ,Sennett Richard .3

.hands your dries it ;thing one do only can that tool a is It .function single a performs it that is problem The .Dryer Hand Airblade his is opinion my in product worst Dyson's

.wasteful is It .progression or development a as classed be cannot ,ugly simply and market the on cleaner vacuum cheapest the as good as only ,weighty overly ,complex overly ,expensive overly is that cleaner vacuum A [2]".it fix don't ,baroque not it's If" ?pioneer a being for lust a with pioneer A

.1991 ,Disney ,*Beast the and Beauty* .2

.improved be to need t'don that ,redesigning need
t'don that things of pioneer a but ,pioneer a is Dyson .need by followed ,simplicity is ,mind my in ,de-
sign good to factor contributing important most
The .masses the of classic unsung the is It .country
the across building government and office council
,cheècr ,station fire ,prison ,station police ,hospital
,school single every in used is it why is This .)part-
ner female pink Henry's – 'Hoover the Hetty' of
case the in chapess happy a or(face chappy happy
smiley a with adorned it's and ,lightweight ,move
to easy ,durable ,compact it's ,hundreds to opposed
as components 40 than more no of up made it's ,ro-
bust more it's .price the of fifth a for sells it although
,Dyson a as suction same the with ,designed perfectly is It .Limited International Numatic by 1981
in introduced ,nickname by 'Hoover the Henry'
,Henry Numatic a is choice of hoover[1] My

.ugly unaccountably is produced has man this
that seen have I everything almost fact In .designer
a not ,engineer an fact in is he ,all after ,forgiven
be can Dyson James Perhaps ?terrible so looks object assembled the ,together pieces those all put you
when come how ,And "?good any be complicated
structurally that something can" :myself to think I
it past walk I time Every .components individual of
hundreds showing ,hoover Dyson disassembled a
is frame Plexiglas a Behind .irritating immensely
find I which ,d'art objet an hangs left the to wall

.Hoover a is it not or whether ,hoover a as to referred is
suction provides that item
lectrical any that deeply
so consciousness British
the penetrated has name
whose rand a is – today
popular ess much although
– today to through 1920s
the from prevalent cleaner
vacuum a ,Hoover .exist
didn't Dyson a ago years
fifteen or ten only perhaps
,itself unto name trade a is
Hoover .HVR200A Henry
Numatic the and Cleaner
Vacuum Bagless Cyclone
Dual Dyson the are names
real whose cleaners vac-
uum identify to 'hoover'
word the mis-use I .1

the on room common senior the in lift the exit you As .afternoon the for themselves prepare to whisky of dram stiff a have can faculty teaching the where place a is It .painting Hockney David a to next hangs painting Freud Lucian a which in bar own its has it that posh frightfully so is room common senior The .crest RCA the with adorned service dinner china fine a and cutlery silver ,cloths table white ,furniture antique with room carpeted ,plush a – room common senior the in luncheon to customary is it London in Art of College Royal the at taught have I When

MUSHROOM KNIFE

A mushroom knife produced by French manufacturer Opinel, featuring a curved blade with a serrated back edge and a boar-hair brush for the removal of soil.

As a child my greatest desire was to one day own a knife of my own. I had no real purpose or need for a knife, but I had an inherent boy scout need to be ever ready. I would spend hours trawling fishing and hunting magazines in our local newsagents, staring at every detail of the many shapes, sizes and possible uses for the knives within. Of course the idea of letting a 10 year-old boy own a real blade was insanity to my parents, and so I was never allowed one. I sufficed with a plastic toy variant, in which a spring loaded blunt grey blade slipped back into the handle, allowing me to merely mimic lethal uses.

During my childhood and teenage years we would take an annual Eurocamp holiday. Eurocamp was a company that catered for middle-class British families who wanted to holiday abroad: camping, caravanning, or occasionally log-cabining amongst other middle-class Britons. The campsites catered for children with kids clubs, swimming pools and other activities, allowing parents to sit in the sun sipping on their rosé wines. It was on one of these holidays that I lost my 'knife virginity'. My brother and I were sitting by a small lake, course-fishing – one of the activities arranged by the Eurocamp reps. Next to us sat a French boy of a similar age. Through our terrible French and his terrible English we exchanged names, he was called Sébastien. Sébastien wore French gym plimsoles, denim cut-off shorts and a long sleeved Breton-striped t-shirt. In his back pocket, to our awe and wonderment, he carried an Opinel penknife. Our parents would only allow us to have a pair of blunt scissors in our fishing kit. The idea that there was a boy out on his own catching fish (for what we imagined was to feed his entire family) with a knife, made our hearts pound with excitement.

During the hours that we sat at the edge of the lake with Sébastien he caught maybe five or six carp, whilst our two rods caught nothing. It was embarrassing. There was a moment, when he realised how suburban we were, that Sébastien decided to lend our useless fishing skills a hand. He walked over to us, casually slipping the wooden handled penknife from his back pocket, unfolded the steel blade and rotated the safety-locking collar mechanism around the handle (to stop the blade from snapping back on his fingers). He marked a square measuring about 20 × 20 cm into the earth, he then cut sideways removing 5 cm of surface soil, leaving what looked like a small tray inset into the ground. He wiped the blade on his cut-off shorts, folded it away and returned it to his back pocket.

He walked down to the water's edge carrying an old tin can that made up part of his humble, make-do fishing kit; filling it with water he carried it back to the square and filled the hole with water. He did this a number of times, each and every time the water being absorbed instantly into the hardened, dry, sun-baked earth. We watched as if he was performing a voodoo ritual, without a clue what was happening. On the fifth water filling exercise we began to see something glisten in the bottom. Sébastien smiled for the first time and looked up with wide eyes trying to communicate the brilliance of his hunter-gatherer skills. Over the next five or ten minutes we pulled 30 or 40 worms from the hole. Sébastien showed us how to hook them onto our fishing lines, replacing the bread balls and sweetcorn our father had given us. We then caught our first fish that day.

Sébastien was our hero and my brother and I would talk about him for years to come as if he was some mythological figure, the epitome of everything that we yearned to be. When my brother and I spoke about him we never called him Sébastien, we referred to him instead as 'Rambo'. It was years later that I realised the beauty of the Opinel knife, partly its wondrous design and simplicity of form, and partly its long, uneventful and enduring history. One of the marvellous things about Opinel knives is their sole purposiveness; the notion that there is a single tool to perform a single job with perfect precision and economy. Much like culinary knife manufacturers – such as the Japanese brand Global, whose range of knives runs into the hundreds – each knife has a slightly different strength, sharpness, thickness, angle, blade size, serration etc. to suit individual food types and uses. In my opinion, the Opinel mushroom knife epitomises this selective and specific function-to-form approach to knife design; it incorporates a brush on the base of its handle to rid the harvest of unwanted soil and has a curved blade for perfectly cutting the stem of the mushroom without damaging its head (despite the fact that foraging for wild mushrooms seems an unpopular activity which couldn't warrant a specific tool).

Today I have a collection of many different knives made by Opinel, each perfectly serving its rightful function: a breadknife, sets of steak knives, a paring knife, a bartenders corkscrew bottle knife and a mushroom knife. I also have a complete collection of the Opinel standard pocket knives in an array of sizes (I'd guess number five was the size of Sébastien's knife). Recently leafing through an Opinel catalogue I came across a newly introduced knife, it caught my attention because its handle was available in a selection of three bright primary colours – unusual for the Opinel brand that usually has a plain, lacquered wood finish. This new knife was rather small, with a rounded tip and a rather blunt blade, as well as having a significantly larger locking mechanism. A knife for children. What a wondrous idea! If only Opinel had thought of that when my brother and I were children, our catch could have fed the entire Eurocamp campsite.

SPRAY PAINT

Two cans of custom-mixed spray paint, one in the traditional Celeste colour (a turquoise also known as 'Bianchi Green') of Bianchi bicycles and the other Hellelfenbein, or Light Ivory, of German taxis.

I suffer from acute colour blindness and would say that the biggest effect it has is to cause an overwhelming sense of doubt. Being colour blind hasn't caused me trouble or infringed upon everyday living, save the slight humiliation in having to ask: "Is this T-shirt green?" or "Are these shoes blue?" I think when you are acutely colour blind you rely on literary language to explain colour as opposed to an innate sensibility. There is a moment in everyone's life during their teenage years where the well-discussed argument of colour recognition theory dawns on them without any real prompting: "If I see this colour as blue and I call it blue and the person beside me sees this colour as green, but they call it blue, what colour is it?" The simple answer to this is that it doesn't matter, it's just that for the person next to you the trees and the grass around them are in fact the colour of what you believe the sky is. The space between neuro-cognitive recognition and verbal identification and communication is a massive abyss that cannot be bridged.

Borne of my doubting of colours, I take great pleasure in RAL codes, Pantone numbers and the descriptive titling of colours by interior decoration paint manufacturers like Dulux or Crown. 'RAL 3004', 'Pantone 256C', 'Whisper of Mellow Sage' or 'Tibetan Gold' leave me with a cheeky smile. Le Corbusier said: "by law all buildings should be white"[1]. I am a huge fan of specific colours that are used solely for one object or brand. Imagine a world where every object had its own hue, it would be boring, but there would be no base for confusion. One of my favourite colours is Bianchi Green, mainly because it doesn't really have a correct RAL code or Pantone reference. An initiative of Bianchi, a bike manufacturer, they primarily mixed and named this colour for copyright reasons so that Bianchi bike frames would have a signature colour and would therefore be more difficult to fake. Bona fide bike re-sprays can only be made at a Bianchi factory.[2] My other favourite sole-purpose colour is the cream that adorns the most omnipresent German private hire cars and taxis. The colour is a vile creamy colour, one that nobody would ever want for their own car. Although it has been the colour of the taxis since 1971, the legislation that demanded all private hire vehicles were this colour was lifted in some jurisdictions in 2005. Not because the colour was disgusting, alas, but because taxis have proven impossible to sell on the second-hand market, as they are continually misidentified as functioning taxis' and re-spraying second-hand cars is simply uneconomical. Imagine, in a world with no rules; Bianchi Green taxis and pukey cream bikes.

1. Possibly from Le Corbusier, *Vers une architecture*, Flammarion, 1923, ill remembered by the author.

2. "There are lots of stories about the true origin of the colour: the colour of the sky in Milan, the colour of the Queen of Italy's eyes, (who Mr Bianchi made a bike for), or from a mix using left over military paints." Writes Phil Mayer, cycling anthropologist.

BLACK PASTA AND WHITSTABLE OYSTERS

A custom-made plate of artificial Spaghetti Nero produced for display purposes. Shown alongside an artificial platter of Whitstable oysters on a bed of artificial ice, produced for presentation purposes.

It is a popular misconception that people eat Spaghetti Nero because of the flavour. Cephalopod ink, or squid ink as it is more commonly known, actually has very little flavour, perhaps a slight taste of brine is all. A squid produces the ink as a defensive reaction when under attack, emitting it in a vast mist, which acts as a smoke screen to enable retreat. Or, mixed with mucus and emitted multiple times within its own vicinity in small clouds, as clones of itself, to divert a predator's attention. When I eat black pasta I often wonder why I ordered it. My thoughts ponder numerous possibilities: do I taste it differently because I see that it's black? Do I know that I am eating ink, the strongest of colourants, associated with permanence, and that affects my taste? Do I eat this as a signifier of my class and refined palate (my black lips and stained teeth surely stand as testament to the fact)? The truth is that I don't like it any more than your average Spaghetti alle Vongole. Perhaps I eat it simply because it is there and I can.

Squid ink was used to write with by the Greeks, but the introduction to Italian cuisine is lost in history. It is possible that it was used to disguise discolouration in fish, as camouflage, similar to the way wasabi and seaweed were used to cloak the taste of rotting sushi fish in Japanese culture. Now enjoyed internationally, but still seen in westernised countries as a bit of an exotic luxury, sushi started out as a nutritional packed lunch for land workers and factory workers, whose inland geography meant that by the time seafood reached them it was likely to be past its best. The introduction of seaweed, ginger and wasabi cloaked the foulness of the rotting fish, whilst the compacted rice balls provided carbohydrates for the workers' energy. It's said that in cities in 19th century Britain the invention of beer and gin and the readiness of its availability and the rise of alcoholism was not so much to do with the escapist properties of alcohol, so much as the fact that it was more sterile and less lethal than the water on offer. With such high incidence of dysentery and plague, alcohol acted as a sanitising component.

Oh how we laughed, the champagne flowed and the oysters were plentiful... I used to eat oysters a lot; my wife and I used to make annual visits to Whitstable, a seaside town in Kent, UK, known for excellent oysters. Since 2008 I have found them quite difficult to enjoy, following a gallery dinner in Amsterdam when I was served an oyster that, as I raised it to my mouth, didn't smell quite right.

I knew as I tipped it into my mouth that I probably shouldn't, but in the formality of the situation I didn't want to seem ungrateful. I blame Britain, ever a nation who finds it hard to complain or send back a dish. The taste was foul, so foul that I did something worse than not eating the oyster in the first place; I spat it back into its shell in front of a table full of people staring at me, mouths agape. The taste was so rancid I knew even a droplet of the water in which the oyster sat would be poisonous. The next day I journeyed from Amsterdam to Bologna to install an exhibition. It was at about three in the afternoon, in a museum press and marketing meeting, when I began to feel strangely light-headed and sweaty. By the time I got back to the hotel I was vomiting and in pain. The curator, Andrea Viliani, a true gentleman and fortunately a friend, went straight to the nearest doctor on my behalf. When he returned a couple of hours later with a miracle cure – a yellow pill, a red pill and a blue pill – I was in the throes of food poisoning, curled on my bed in agony, sweating profusely and suffering from hallucinations that my brother was in the room talking to me about fly-fishing, describing the best cast-line to use on still water. As Andrea explained to me the order and times I should take the technicolour pharmaceuticals, his words slowed and morphed like the soundtrack of The Beatles' *Magical Mystery Tour.* This food poisoning was like LSD. It took me three days to recover and I swore I would never touch another oyster again.

Since that episode I've paid special attention to any story I've come across involving an oyster. I revel in the contradictions surrounding oysters: delicacy/foodstuff for the masses and aphrodisiac/poisoner. Although today oysters are seen as an extravagance enjoyed by the affluent, historically oysters were a food for the poor and the working class – a cheap source of sustenance that were readily available, plucked from the sea by children. So many old English recipes incorporated oysters (steak and oyster pie, potted shrimp and oysters, or pike and oyster stew, for examples) because they were good sources of protein in the otherwise poor nutritional diets of factory and land workers; they could be freely plucked from the sea; and so long as they weren't transported too far, their freshness was guaranteed. I now make a point of enjoying a pint of ale with a platter of oysters, instead of a bottle of white wine, as a nod to the story of class conflict that oysters carry, like conceptual vessels. Last year I read in a national paper that the annual crop of Whitstable oysters had failed. Unbalancing the economy and putting a huge number of jobs in jeopardy, hundreds of thousands of oysters were being disposed of in landfill due to a previously unknown strain of a virus. Later in the article it described that the nearest known disease to which the oysters predicament could be compared was that of herpes, the sexually transmitted disease occurring in humans. What a beautifully poetic contradiction: oysters, regarded an aphrodisiac, suffering from a sexually transmitted disease. There was, to my mind, no image more comically poignant with as much significance in its contradiction, as the image of a beautiful young couple staring into each other's eyes across a candlelit table, white table cloth, bottle of champagne, arms crossed over fine china, each holding aloft a shell, feeding each other the world's most treasured aphrodisiac. Not only sharing their love for each other, but sharing oyster herpes.

ZIPPO PERFUME

A 30 ml refillable eau de toilette spray bottle of the scent Zippo Original for men by the same company that manufactures Zippo lighters. The perfume is housed in a bottle resembling a Zippo lighter with a nozzle to expel the perfume that resembles a burning wick.

The manufacturing of Zippo lighter fluid and Zippo petrol lighters dates back to the Second World War, with its origins in military usage. The recent development within the company into the production of men's fragrances, perfumes and eau de toilette is a perfect example of the trend for the increasing significance of branding and the decreasing significance of product. The beauty of this example lies in the clumsy collision between Zippo's manufacture of two flammable products: one, a liquid to burn which smells atrocious; and two, a liquid applied to the skin to make you smell good. The fragrance is ludicrously presented in packaging that mimics an original Zippo petrol lighter, and yet it sells. It is widely available in department stores all over Europe and the USA. Branding aside, its marketing conjures 'the Zippo man', similar to the 'Marlboro Man': a strong, rugged, outdoorsman, a hunter-gatherer, immune to the elements and immune to smoking related diseases. The fragrance is bought, not for its bouquet, but for the desire for strength and increased masculinity. On the subject of the aroma, it is of a distinctly substandard category of fragrances on the market; it lacks subtlety, originality and a layering of undertones. It can be herded into the same pen as Brut, Lynx, Old Spice and Badedas; fragrances that are sold in cheaper outlets and relegated to one underdog shelf in department stores. Zippo's smell is noxious and overpowering – a quality that might be an asset when you consider that its end user is most likely a keen smoker.

There is an increasing gap in consumer consciousness between the fame of a brand and the excellence of a product. One could speculate that it's associated with a working-class consumer who is captivated by the strength and immediacy of the identity, in opposition to the complexities and high costs of finely crafted products that have history as their reference and a signature of excellence. An absurd result of brands expanding into other unrelated product markets is the damage to those brands' classic ranges, for which the company has been built and is traditionally known for producing. A good example is the pornographic brand, Playboy, which has filtered down and across (admittedly in part by society's increasing tolerance towards nudity) varied market places to a point today where 8 year-old daughters beg their parents for Playboy pencil cases in supermarket stationery aisles. Ferrari is another example, especially in Italian culture, where the supercar giant now makes thousands and thousands of everyday products. As if owning a Ferrari key ring, pair of trainers or record bag would assist you in reaching incredible speeds on a racing track without actually owning a Ferrari itself. It raises the question: do Ferrari propelling pencils, jotters and such like, match the excellence in quality that one would expect from a Ferrari? I'm sure the answer is no. I'm pretty sure the propelling pencil will break, the jeans will split at the seams, the soles of the trainers hold no grip, the zip on the pencil case snags and becomes unaligned, the colours of the bed spreads fade and I'm left with an aroma of lighter fluid surrounding me.

A silk scarf designed and produced by the artist, with a pattern consisting of reproductions of the artist's collection of perfume sample strips, on each of which is written the name of the perfume as well as name of the airport and city where it was acquired.

I have a project that has inched along in its development at a painfully slow snail's pace. The work, to be entitled 'The Corporate Tear' (2012) is now in its fourth year of production, having initially been intended from completion in 2008. The idea is simple: a ladies' scarf measuring 90 × 90 cm, made from 100% silk, with imagery of a vast array of perfume swatches I have collected from airports around the world. Each perfume swatch has been sprayed in the duty-free section of the airport, then the names of the perfume, airport and city are written on each swatch. They have been scanned and placed on a black background, printed onto the scarf in a random composition. The beauty of the project, to my mind, is that the currency of most garments of this nature is in the display of the name or logo of the brand. On my scarf you see the logos of Dior, Chanel, Boots the Chemist and Thierry Mugler (among many others) on the swatches and so the multiplicity of the scarf's provenance becomes a contradiction, deconstructing the semiotics of fashion labelling. The scarf is also a diary tracking my movements around the globe in relation to the exhibiting of my work. The purposeful confusion of the scarf's provenance also leads us to a conceptual deceit: the viewer's inability to use their sense of smell to experience the swatches. If the scarf were made of paper and silk and incorporated actual perfume swatches, it would emit a deadly stench, akin to the one that hits you as you enter the perfume section of a department store. It's an amalgamation of every type of perfume you can think of, which produces a smell comparable, in aural terms, to the noise that would be emitted if every electrical appliance in your house were switched on simultaneously. I revel in the idea that a wearer may question or forget its materiality and attempt, in a brief moment of confusion, to sniff the Viktor & Rolf perfume strip to remind herself of the fragrance. Mmmmmmm… the smell of silk.

The problems with the project and the reasons for its lengthy production have been largely logistical, things that made themselves apparent over time: the quality of the reverse ink penetration on some fabrics using some printing methods was poor, meaning that the colours are muted and dull; the text showed through the thin silk and was therefore reversed and so on. There is the predicament of financial viability: as an artist it would make sense for it to be a unique artwork, but for it to function in the way it is conceptually intended it must be worn by many. It will function most eloquently and intelligently when distributed widely, entering the world on an equal footing with other fashion garments, sitting uncomfortably alongside a Hermès scarf for example; like a tongue-in-cheek, bastardised version of the intentions of such counterparts. And finally the problem of copyright: an issue of endless concern to conceptual artists whose practices toy with socio-cultural positions of objects in the world. A specialist copyright lawyer I consulted has recommended that reproducing corporate fashion house logos onto a garment to be sold for profit is a naïve idea. For the moment I am happy with numerous prototypes of differing sizes, qualities, compositions, designs and content. But I still have an itch to move forwards.

DYSON FAN

A Dyson bladeless Air Multiplier 10 inch desk fan in the colours iron and blue.

When I have taught at the Royal College of Art in London it is customary to luncheon in the senior common room – a plush, carpeted room with antique furniture, white table cloths, silver cutlery and a fine china dinner service adorned with the RCA crest. The senior common room is so frightfully posh that it has its own bar in which a Lucian Freud painting hangs next to a David Hockney painting. It is a place where the teaching faculty can have a stiff dram of whisky to prepare themselves for the afternoon. As you exit the lift in the senior common room on the wall to the left hangs an objet d'art, which I find immensely irritating. Behind a Plexiglas frame is a disassembled Dyson hoover, showing hundreds of individual components. Every time I walk past it I think to myself: "can something that structurally complicated be any good?" And, how come when you put all those pieces together, the assembled object looks so terrible? Perhaps James Dyson can be forgiven, after all, he is in fact an engineer, not a designer. In fact almost everything I have seen that this man has produced is unaccountably ugly.

My hoover[1] of choice is a Numatic Henry, 'Henry the Hoover' by nickname, introduced in 1981 by Numatic International Limited. It is per-

1. I mis-use the word 'hoover' to identify vacuum cleaners whose real names are the Dyson Dual Cyclone Bagless Vacuum Cleaner and the Numatic Henry HVR200A. Hoover is a trade name unto itself, perhaps only ten or

fectly designed, with the same suction as a Dyson, although it sells for a fifth of the price. It's more robust, it's made up of no more than 40 components as opposed to hundreds, it's compact, durable, easy to move, lightweight, and it's adorned with a smiley happy chappy face (or a happy chapess in the case of 'Hetty the Hoover' – Henry's pink female partner). This is why it is used in every single school, hospital, police station, prison, fire station, crèche, council office and government building across the country. It is the unsung classic of the masses. The most important contributing factor to good design, in my mind, is simplicity, followed by need. Dyson is a pioneer, but a pioneer of things that don't need redesigning, that don't need to be improved. A pioneer with a lust for being a pioneer? "If it's not baroque, don't fix it."[2] A vacuum cleaner that is overly expensive, overly complex, overly weighty, only as good as the cheapest vacuum cleaner on the market and simply ugly, cannot be classed as a development or progression. It is wasteful.

Dyson's worst product in my opinion is his Airblade Hand Dryer. The problem is that it performs a single function. It is a tool that can only do one thing; it dries your hands.

fifteen years ago a Dyson didn't exist. Hoover, a vacuum cleaner prevalent from the 1920s through to today – although much less popular today – is a brand whose name has penetrated the British consciousness so deeply that any electrical item that provides suction is referred to as a hoover, whether or not it is a Hoover.

2. *Beauty and the Beast*, Disney, 1991.

The all-purpose tool seems a special case. In a piano maker's cabinet, the flat edged screwdriver comes close to being such a tool, since it can gouge, lift, and line as well as screw. But in its sheer variety this all-purpose tool admits all manner of unfathomed possibilities; it, too, can expand our skills if only our imagination rises to the occasion.[3]

3. Richard Sennett, *The Craftsman*, Penguin, 2008, p. 198.

The Dyson Airblade replaces hand dryers more similar in style to those produced by American Dryer, Inc. Physically the Dyson is four times larger than the tool it is replacing. It is not as good looking as its predecessor; it looks like something that has broken off the Starship Enterprise. The Airblade does dry the hands of its user several seconds faster than the object it is replacing, but that's all it does. Countless times I have washed my face in a public bathroom. The ingenious design of the standard hand dryer is that the nozzle that directs the air down to your hands can be turned upside down so that the airstream is directed into the face or the hair; giving the tool a second and third use (and a fourth if you count its ability to dry clothes after stain and rain emergencies). Not only does the Airblade suffer from a singular use, it is one of the noisiest hand dryers on the market. It also uses a vast amount of electricity and is the most unhygienic hand dryer on the market; the water that is pushed from your hands collects in a crevasse where two pieces of plastic meet at the bottom and there it sits, perhaps evaporating into the humidity of the toilet, perhaps dribbling down the side of the hand dryer, or perhaps leaking into the large casing below the Airblade aperture. Where is this water meant to go?

I've recently purchased a Dyson fan, an 'Air Multiplier'. The annoying thing is it's actually quite good. Especially if you have kids because they can't stick their fingers in the blades as there aren't any. Compared to a regular bladed fan, it's simple, economical, more power efficient, silent, easy to clean, easy to store and moves a greater amount of air. In the beginning I thought it was a fad, but I like it. And it looks quite good too.

DUNWICH AIR

A vintage glass bell jar sealed to its wooden base with silicone, containing sea air from the small town of Dunwich not far from the artist's house in Suffolk. Fifteen hundred years ago Dunwich was the capital of East Anglia but the harbour and much of the original town have since disappeared due to coastal erosion, remaining intact yet inaccessible under the North Sea.

There's a coastal place 15 minutes drive North from my house called Dunwich. In the Domesday Book of 1086, Dunwich was recorded as the capital of Suffolk, a thriving port with a population of 3000. Nowadays Dunwich is little more than a pub, a tiny two-room museum and a car park. The town now lies under the sea due to coastal erosion, which had been effective over the years because of the local geology and the strength of the North Sea tidal patterns.

I've heard stories told in local pubs about the ghosts of Dunwich that rise up from the ocean: of how you can see the eight spires of the churches of Dunwich protruding from the horizon during low tides, and of how you can still hear the ghostly ring of the church bells. There's always romanticism for towns that once were and are no longer, for the fact that they are still preserved, like a moment in time, albeit unobtainable to the human eye, like Dunwich or Pompeii.

One summer's day journeying around the neighbouring villages in the Suffolk countryside, I came across a bell jar in an antiques shop. The price led me to believe that it was not antique, although it had an 'antique feel'. The problem with such display devices is that they are usually more appealing than the objects inside. Or, at least the object on display has to live up to the worthy form of presentation. It occurred to me that it might be nice to take the jar to Dunwich and fill it with air on the sea front, seal it with silicone bathroom sealer and bring it home to display in our house. The jar now acts as a constant reminder of how lucky we are to live in such a beautiful county by the sea, as well as the luxury of no longer having to hare around mindlessly with other city-dwellers.

Recently it also reminded me of a text I once read when I was a student. I can't recall the name now but it was written by the French author André Gide and it was somehow related to the notion that fish float[1]. I think the reasoning was that if a zero point when we die is the ground, we are then traditionally buried beneath the ground. Whereas a reverse logic can be applied to fish because they swim beneath the horizon but float up to it when they die. I remember jokingly musing over why the mouths of some fish were above their eyes when I read this quote. It also occurred to me that if either of these reasonings were true it would mean

1. The quote goes something like: "Fish die belly upward, and rise to the surface. It's their way of falling".

that fish as we visually know them could be considered permanently upside down. When I combine these three stories in my head now, looking at my bell jar full of Dunwich air, it occurs to me that the jar should in fact be full of water from the North Sea. There is probably space for another bell jar next to the original, containing water from the North Sea as well as a tiddler swimming around upside down.

LEICA M9

A Leica M9 digital camera, the latest model in the series of rangefinder cameras produced by the German optics company since 1923. It propels the legendary Leica M cameras into the digital age and is the smallest full-format digital system camera the world has ever seen.

I have frequently been known to make clear my disdain for artists who are interested in the idea of being an artist more than in the idea of the production of art. When I am asked what my occupation is I sometimes reply that I am a teacher, especially when being asked by a cab driver whose viewpoint on the artworld – however stereotypical and prejudiced this may sound – is one of skepticism and critique. No artist wants to get into a discussion with a cab driver about contemporary art. And besides, it's not a lie; I do teach, although making art is my primary occupation.

The lifestyle of an artist and being characterised as an artist do not appeal to me, but making art does. Recently I realised a huge contradiction in my view on this. I have always wanted to be a reportage photographer, though it's not the work that appeals to me (running around Afghanistan taking photos of dead bodies, or shooting candid portraits from the hip at Ascot aren't activities that I want to be involved in). Instead I'm interested in being a photographer, steeped in all its romanticism, stereotype and nostalgia. As if being a photographer would enhance my quality of life; the idea of waking up in a grainy world in which I was a turtle-neck sweater clad, full-head-of-haired, womanising, Gauloises-smoking, Campari-drinking, educated, eloquent, handsome stop-out. A photographer, who in many respects is a god, with an ability to immortalise others with the release of a shutter. If I were this sepia-toned demi-god my tool of choice would be a Leica. A simple rangefinder camera made by a German optics company formerly known as Ernst Leitz GmbH, established in 1913 and now based in Solms, Germany.

The Leica M9 camera, which is the modern digital version of the classic that has marked our history, is incredibly expensive. The body and a lens are priced in the region of £8,000, making it desirable not merely for its history, quality and retro, simple good looks, but also its value as a luxury commodity. It is this that really interests me. If you do an internet image search for the Leica M9 there are almost as many images of people looking through the viewfinder of a Leica as there are of the Leica itself. What are we looking for here? An image produced by a Leica camera, an image of a Leica camera, or an image of the owner of a Leica camera being immortalised with their Leica camera? Owners of Leica cameras get tetchy when you ask if you can have a go. The idea that the viewfinder of their

Leica is up against another person's eye seems unthinkable.

In many respects the camera acts as a division, clearly separating and defining two distinct and contrary roles: the eye that looks through the viewfinder (with the intention of capturing an image); and the eye that looks into the lens (with the intention of having an image captured). Similarly, when you use a camera you look through it from the back, out onto the world in front of you (a very external operation). But when you look at a camera, you look into it from the front, with its operator behind observing you placed in the world (a very internal operation).

The Leica is not only a tool to do a job, but also an accessory to support the image of a photographer who is happy to be identified as 'a photographer'. The archetypal image here being that of the photographer pictured with their camera, akin to the semiotics of the Victorian seaside pier: an invention of a journey without destination, the only function of which is the futile promenade for walking to see and be seen as a signifier of status. The currency of the Leica is the status in its visibility. To aid in the photographer's struggle for identification, the Leica M9 is a wise and obvious choice.

MACARON

Macarons in the customised flavours of Foie Gras, burning libraries and Evian mineral water, prepared at the behest of the artist.

Rose Watkins-Jones: Why macarons?

Ryan Gander: Three reasons, starting with the fact that I ate a macaron for the first time only last year. You've probably been eating them for years, it turned out my friends had. It made me feel inexperienced, like I had been missing out on something that everyone kept secret from me. It's amazing to discover something that has been around for years and you were simply unaware of, especially at the age of 36. Secondly, I was awestruck by the array of flavours macarons come in and by how the colour combinations of each macaron represented the flavour, making them easy to identify. This got me thinking about flavours that weren't available, and flavours that could be possible. The third reason was that I was (embarrassingly) impressed by their luxury; they seem to belong to a world of small boutiques in cosmopolitan cities, populated by posh older ladies dripping with jewels. Their luxury is also reflected in their tiny size to preparation time and skill ratio.

RWJ: Why did you choose macarons rather than macaroons?

RG: I mistakenly called them macaroons [a different type of confectionary made with coconut] after I first discovered them actually... macaroons are a bit scally, no? They sell them in Iceland supermarkets? Macarons are for the sophisticated.

RWJ: Can I ask you what the 'burning libraries' flavour is about?

RG: I was trying to think of themed macarons – not only plausible ones – which you would imagine to be impossible to make. The burning libraries flavour macaron is a bit like special edition Quality Street at Christmas, or McVitie's biscuits in a Jubilee celebration tin; it's a commemorative revolutionary themed one for the Ancient Library of Alexandria, Egypt, that Julius Caesar accidentally burned down in 48 BC.

RWJ: Why did you choose to change the flavours of macarons instead of the shapes, for example?

RG: Thinking about it as a real macaron in the shape of an Evian bottle, a model of a burning library and a slab of Foie Gras would have done a similar job and would have been interesting, but perhaps it would have been too believable. If I showed you those, you wouldn't doubt that they were actual cake; you wouldn't spend very long thinking about it; you wouldn't wonder, mull and imagine. I think one of the roles of art is to provoke the viewer to think and to question what is in front of them. The way it is, the macarons are confusing enough to hold your attention, for a while anyway.

RWJ: Are they actually for people to eat or are they just art? Are you concerned about the taste?

RG: I love the fact that you say "just" art! Although you are right, real, edible macarons probably do have more worth to us than my plastic inedible ones. The truth is, of course, that they don't taste of anything (except plastic). They are, and I say this defeated, fakes... It is most likely impossible to get Evian flavouring, after all what does water taste of? I am concerned about the taste, but only the space between us imagining and experiencing the taste. I wanted to make something unbelievable, but at the same time enticing enough to motivate you to imagine the taste. I knew you wouldn't believe they were real!

(An interview on the subject of macarons, by Rose Watkins-Jones, aged 15.)

SECURITY MIRROR

A circular convex security mirror with protective visor intended for outdoor use, manufactured in Japan.

I've been trying to work out if I spend more time looking in mirrors at other people's reflections than I do looking at my own reflection. We assume that we most often use mirrors as tools to examine our own reflections, but I'm not sure this is true when I think about how much time I spend looking in the rear-view and wing mirrors of my car. The security mirror, is another deviation from self-gazing – its function, in an idealistic sense, is to view the reflection of nobody. These mirrors are used to check that there is no person lurking in a secluded space, around a corner, in a lift foyer, in an underground car park, or between shop aisles. When installed for drivers, security mirrors are used for checking that there are no oncoming vehicles when pulling out of hidden side-roads or driveways. In a perverse relationship the dynamics between the spectator, the spectacle and viewing device are muddled: we are given the opportunity to look so that we can see a non-spectacle.

The convex nature of the security mirror has other significant historic and cultural repercussions; in 'The Arnolfini Portrait' (1434), by Jan van Eyck, we are reminded that the convex mirror is not an all-seeing eye, but a shared eye. In van Eyck's painting it is the eye of the artist, the eye of the sitter and the eye of us, the spectator. I love this work, I love it as an unwitting precursor to conceptual art, it portrays a super loop of meaning seemingly far ahead of its time.

The convex mirror is also the main totemic symbol of the Dazaifu Tenman-gū Shinto shrine in Fukuoka – a shrine where visitors are left open to freely interpret the spiritual significance of both objects and buildings. It is, if you will, a shrine based on a religion with a blank sheet of paper on which you can write your own personal motivations for belief. It is quite interesting therefore that this 'all seeing' convex vessel, or porthole, to an imagined elsewhere is its emblem. As if to suggest that the believer is given the privileged ability to view the designated or imagined god or religious figure, and vice versa. As if belief was an exchange as opposed to an investment.

An arrangement of Vajazzles (glitter and crystal jewel stickers that are applied to women's genitals and bikini areas for aesthetic purposes) presented on a lifelike mannequin's body.

The word 'vajazzle' entered common English language in 2010, as a compound of the words 'vagina' and 'bedazzle'. 'Vajazzle' describes the act of decorating a woman's genital area with tiny, colourful, self-adhesive crystals, usually in a triangular shape, where one usually finds pubic hair (which, in the case of vajazzling, has been stripped bare to enable its replacement with the decorative crystals). More often than not in documented designs, vajazzling takes the form of a triangle with a rounded top, unintentionally representing a partially opened fan, with a pattern of striped colours that radiate from the lower point. This design also seems to act as a large arrow pointing towards the vagina. Associations can be made here to the peacock's plume, not only in the shape of the display, but also in the idea that each of these tiny crystals represents an all-seeing-eye, like the ocelli in peacock feathers. The primary function of a peacock's open plumage is sexual, a show of prowess to attract a mate. Vajazzling unwittingly mimics this, but logically the display is directed at someone who is already a sexual partner, otherwise vajazzles would be (inappropriately and perhaps illegally) on public display to attract mates.

Recently I came across another '...azzle': a 'pejazzle'. The decoration of the penis with tiny self-adhesive crystals. Both pejazzling and vajazzling leave me confused, pejazzling especially makes me frightened, conjuring images of bejewelled serpents, lost in mis-meaning without context nor reason for existence. The packaging of the vajazzles that I purchased for my research purposes bears the slogan: 'Bling for your private parts'. 'Bling' itself was introduced into the *Oxford English Dictionary* only nine years ago, its definition reading:

> **Bling**
>
> **Pronunciation**: /blɪŋ/ (also bling-bling)
>
> ***informal noun*** [mass noun]
>
> expensive, ostentatious clothing and jewellery: *look at the bling he's already wearing on his left arm*
>
> ***adjective***
>
> denoting expensive, ostentatious clothing or jewellery, or the style or materialistic attitudes associated with them: *the bling lifestyle of diamond rings, flashy cars, and champagne*

To my mind, bling is associated with what was an aspiring working class ten years ago and is now a middle class of the semi nouveau riche, whose primary concern is a quest for a display of wealth, whether it be actual or deluded, and an obsession with consumerism and the rich and famous. The notion of bling can be seen to resonate through contemporary British culture in a self-fulfilling, self-fuelling circle of cause and effect: the diamond-studded skull of Damien Hirst, "The rocks" J-Lo "got", 50 Cent's autobiographical album *Get Rich Or Die Trying*, pink Range Rovers in *The Only Way Is Essex* and such like do nothing but exacerbate the situation. And so it seems that this showy, faux display of wealth has filtered down, through media and popular culture, through the class stratification system across Britain, into the underwear of young women across the nation, manifesting itself on their vajayjays.

RECORD TURNING ROUND

A 7 inch vinyl record of the song 'Turning Round' by Chris de Burgh.

I once wrote an article for one of those music magazines, so specialist that most of us would not recognise the name of a single musician.[1] I've always had an aversion to the subculture of music, not the music nor its production, but the appreciation of it: the geeky fetishism of the obscure, the thirst for rare recordings, B-sides, hidden tracks and bootlegs. I love music, my collection is broad and sizeable. I am knowledgeable about the history of many of the bands I like, their discographies and the affiliations between different bands. These simply aren't things that I feel the need to share with other music appreciators.

There is elitism in music subculture that victimises those whose taste touches upon popular music genres (one might also encounter the same thing when going into a high-end cycle shop with a wheelchair puncture, or visiting a professional camera shop to ask about a pocket digital). The article I wrote for the magazine incorporated my views on this elitism, namely there are tracks and albums in my collection by artists that music magazine readers would frown upon, chuckle at, or even be astonished by. Tracks that I listen to regularly that I'm not ashamed of, including the likes of Chris de Burgh, Tracy Chapman, The Levellers, and Dire

1. *The Wire* #310, December 2009, The Inner Sleeve: Ryan Gander on Neil Young's *On The Beach*.

Straits. I am aware of the historical and cultural references, implications and stigmas associated with these artists. I know where they come from. I know how the artists came into being and I've lived in the world at the moment they arrived in it. For me my appreciation is musical, I don't listen to these artists ironically and I don't listen to them to champion the out-dated, forgotten, ridiculed bygones of previous chart success. I listen to them because I enjoy it. I am not tarred by the snobbery of muso-ponces.

'Turning Round' (1976) is a beautiful song by Chris de Burgh, a British/Irish singer songwriter born in 1948, most well known for his love ballad, 'Lady in Red' (1986) which reached number one in six countries. It's a song in my record collection that I often return to and it's a song that makes people cringe with embarrassment when they hear it for the first time, but a song they always end up singing along to. I chose 'Turning Round' as an example of a song that is wonderful, but loathed. Then I realised that the title descriptively identi fies the movement of the record itself as an object. That's one thing that records always do, regardless of cultural baggage. Even Black Lace's 'Agadoo'. Let them turn.

Ten letters written by the artist to ten individuals of significant wealth and cultural merit, frankly requesting financial support to purchase a derelict Victorian school in a small town in the English countryside where the artist lives, and to transform it into a private residency, art school and research centre.

I am intrigued by the notion of the art school and its potential for change. I am no expert, but having attended many, in the capacities of both student and tutor, as well as participating and working on the development of new educational models, I can say I know a bit about them. The idea of an artist running an art school is not a new idea, in fact every great movement and trajectory in the history of contemporary art has come through artists meddling in the idea of education. From Black Mountain College to the Bauhaus, and to more current examples like Olafur Eliasson's Institute for Spatial Experiments (a title oozing with pseudo-intellectuality, over-complicating and mystifying what is basically a degree in architectural art).

Alongside the artist-led educational initiatives there are countless groups of artists who have produced educational manifestos, outlining and optimising direction or objectives for practice: The Futurists, Fischli/Weiss, Art & Language, to name but a few. My favourite manifesto for practicing artists is entitled *I Am for an Art* by Claes Oldenburg and takes the form of several pages of singular sentences each starting with: "I am for an art..." the most memorable to me being: "I am for an art that is a conversation between the blind man's stick and the pavement."[1] An ex-tutor of mine called Dave Smith once said to me: "The best art school can simply be a warm room." I think these two statements by Oldenburg and Smith perfectly instill my beliefs in what an art education should be. I believe you learn more from those who are naturally around you rather than those who are placed around you 'to teach'. And, no matter how extensive an individual's opportunities, privileges and education, these pale in comparison to ingenuity and energy for self-initiated activities. I think David Hockney sums it all up with the words: "Inspiration? She never visits the lazy."[2]

When visiting art schools around the world (which I always say I must stop, due to my studio workload, but which I always agree to neverthe less) I meet numerous students from various backgrounds all in various life predicaments. The most excruciating are probably the trustafarian rich kids, whose security is a given and for whom enrolling into art school provides a hobby for life and the meeting of a cultured set. There are often the students who make wax moulds of their bodies; the ones making work about their brothers that died

1. Claes Oldenburg, *I Am for an Art* (1961) from: Charles Harrison and Paul Wood, *Art in Theory. 1900-1990: An Anthology of Changing Ideas*, Blackwell, 1992, pp. 727-730.

2. http://www.tate.org.uk/tateshots

in car accidents; the ones playing with 16 mm film because they like the vintage feel of the media; the street artists; the mature students who are obsessed with imagined constructions of beauty and craft; the ones who make videos spreading black cherries on their breasts; and the ones who singe the edges of photographs and stain them with tea. More often than not, and quite naturally, almost all the students are phony, but once in a blue moon I come across an individual whose work astonishes me, which is accompanied by a slight jealousy in the pit of my stomach. It's a good jealousy; to know that someone ten years my junior has got to a place that I'd like to be in is a slap round the face that leaves me eager to get back to the studio. I would claim (though it sounds like an idiotic stereotype) that these students are most often from unprivileged backgrounds: northern town-dwellers, working-class terraces, broken and uncultured families. I don't know why this is but I'm sure it has less to do with understanding visual language and more to do with the fact that out of these backgrounds come strong, self-reliant, resourceful and entrepreneurial characters.

Recently my wife pointed out to me a Victorian school that was up for sale in the small town where we live in Suffolk. The school, structurally sound but in need of some modernisation, is available at a greatly reduced price for a future public usage, as opposed to demolishing it and building twat-flats. I'm not sure if it was because my wife has always known of my idea to start an art school or if opening one in our small town would ensure I was at home more, but she definitely, deviously planted the seed in my head. It wouldn't really be an art school, it would be a residency program, and it would be self-sustainable by making the rooms and studios available to rent for three months during the summer. The school, which I might call 'The All-Striped Artists' Academy of Contemporary Practice', would house seven artists with live/work studios. It would also have a communal dining room and kitchen, a gallery open to the public three days a week, an arts library open to the public by appointment, a digital media workshop, a mess shop for sculpture construction, and a small auditorium. The school would need an office for two staff (a program director and a technical director) as well as three humble guest quarters for visiting participants and advisors to stay.

The best things about the town are that it's only two hours from London by train or just over two hours drive on a single straight road, it's by the sea, and in a region peppered with the residence of significant historical and contemporary artists. The town is remote enough to enable concentration without distraction, yet it has all necessary amenities: hotel, pub, post office, supermarket, art and craft supply shop, bookshop, deli etc. The academic programme would be unstructured; one day per week there would be two or three visiting practitioners with whom the residents could talk if they wished. The visitors, chosen by the residents themselves, would be offered a place to stay and a communal meal. Once a year there would be a symposium; the remit of which would be left as open as possible for the residents to define. The most important thing would be that they are given time and space, and that any real activity or movement into the public domain came from the heart of the school itself, the resident artists rather than the administrative direction.

I think I need about £2,000,000 to cover the costs of building renovation, two staff for a three-year period, setting up the programme and time to raise further funds to run into the future. It all seems ideal, save the £2,000,000 I don't have. I do have my aspiration and energy for self-initiated activity, so perhaps I do have £2,000,000 but I just don't know it yet.

MILLIGANHAND MAGNETS

Alphabet magnets made in the typeface 'Milliganhand', invented by the artist using the handwriting of Spike Milligan. Displayed here on a small refrigerator.

As a child my father often read to me a book of poetry and prose to assist in the lengthy process of falling asleep. It was written by the comedian, broadcaster, writer, radio journalist and public speaker Spike Milligan. The only poem I know by heart in the world is 'The Baboon' by Spike Milligan, which appeared in his book *Silly Verse for Kids* (1959).

There was a baboon
Who one afternoon
Said "I think I shall fly to the sun."
So with two great palms
Strapped to his arms
He started his takeoff run.

Mile after mile
He galloped in style
But never once left the ground.
"You're running too slow"
Said a passing crow,
"Try reaching the speed of sound."

So he put on a spurt-
By God how it hurt!

The soles of his feet caught fire.
There were great clouds of steam
As he ran through a stream
But he still didn't get any higher.

Racing on through the night
Both his knees caught alight
And smoke billowed out from his rear.
Quick to his aid
Came a Fire Brigade
Who chased him for over a year.

Many moons passed by.
Did Baboon ever fly?
Did he ever get to the sun?
I've just heard today
That he's well on his way!
He'll be passing through Acton at one.

Brilliantly comic as well as excruciatingly intelligent. Both my brother and I spent years falling asleep with imagery conjured by Milligan's poems spinning like whirlwinds in our imaginations and elbowing their way into our dreams. Not only an accomplished writer but also an intellectual with a jaw-droppingly inventive mind, Milligan took every brief and treatment as a challenge, thinking creatively and laterally about his responses. When requested by the BBC to write an introduction for the inlay card for a recording of *The Goon Show* – a comedy written and enacted by himself alongside Harry Secombe and Peter Sellers – Milligan responded with the following text:

> *The BBC have asked me to write a hundred and fifty words to go along with this cassette. Fish, love cupboard / ripe, leg, pencil, house, nail, teeth, kiss, flute, elephant / giant, honey, rabbit, scouse, lamp, whistle, cup, clarionet / horse, grain, Poona, rust, gutter, plimsole, hurt, dental / client, musket, plinth, calf, mutton, if, no, but, fish / nun, broom, bail, cliff, age, Kenneth, cab, slur, angle / pin, dent, plinth, dog, ease, ear, lentil, nose, grey, desert, lino, glint, earth, dial, hair, dirt, porridge, note / court, cannon, live, ant, garment, spook, cannon, diet, coke, oil, bustard, gannet, net, spice, lemon. guitar, string. dote, domt, minute, sterile, saint / ranger, moon, coat, nether, lint, stamp, hand, oats, noon, kitten, earth, tea, party, lemon, lute, gong / priest nonsense pickle brain, curve, rick, nest*, dog / easy fox. bolt, second, honk, doubt, curtain lid / ache, axle. dolt, pun, liver, tin, milk, oboe, pink, ton* / wheel, buck, norman. dive, trap, trot, poke, pig pound, lentil, soup, trundle, trap, ink, wad, tick, flute, note* / telegraph, cart, bullock, pack, forage, cut, tin, lid, egg, seam, torrent, roger, vault, item, itch.*
>
> **used twice for effect.*[1]

1. *Box 18: The Unpublished Spike Miligan*, Fourth Estate, 2006.

After my daughter Olive was born it occurred to me that I would like to introduce the Spike Milligan references to her psyche, as my father had to mine. When I began to read Milligan poems to her as a 1 year-old it didn't make sense as she was too young; she needed to be a little older to appreciate the juxtaposition of colliding ideas. It occurred to me that I should make her an object to play with that would represent the characteristics of Milligan's work, whilst allowing her to be creative, rather than reading, repeating, learning and appreciating as I did.

One luxury of having art as your principal occupation is the necessity of a studio; a multi-faceted space containing adaptable tools and adaptable, intelligent people. With this luxury comes the privilege of being able to have a multitude of things fabricated or produced. I went about having a set of fridge magnets made for my daughter, cut from sandblasted Plexiglas to adorn them with a matt frosted finish, in bright primary colours. The characters were cut from a fully functioning typeface that I invented and produced with the logistical help of my friend Rasmus Spanggaard Troelsen, a type designer with the determination of a shire horse. The typeface is called 'Milliganhand' and is a generalised typeface based on the handwriting of the late Spike Milligan, each character made up from a simplified outline of the average shape of three or four examples of each letter.

It was a seemingly nice idea whose full potential made itself apparent in retrospect. One of the most wondrous things about Milligan – and the main reason I am obsessed with him – was his work as a neologist, an inventor of words. Milligan invented several hundred words over the course of his career (akin to Theodor Seuss Geisel, more commonly known as Dr. Seuss, who also introduced his invented words into his children's books). In context on our fridge door at home, the 'Milliganhand' magnets sit quietly camouflaged amongst postcards, shopping lists and family photographs. Over time, through their usage, the magnets have brought out the neologist in my daughter and myself, although at aged three many of her arrangements don't make pronounceable words. It's a game with no objective, a game with no rules, a game that champions nonsense – ideologies that I believe would have warmed Milligan's heart.

MORRIS' SATCHEL

A reconstruction of William Morris' satchel, the original of which is housed at the William Morris Gallery in Walthamstow, UK. Morris is said to have distributed socialist leaflets from the satchel.

In the mid-'90s I was in a group exhibition at the ICA, London, in which I wanted to exhibit an article lent from William Morris Gallery, Walthamstow. The museum wouldn't loan me the article in question even though the conditions of conservation at the ICA were more than adequate for the exhibit. There was no explanation as to why. Instead I made a work where the invigilator was instructed to read the futuristic utopian arts and crafts tale, *News From Nowhere* (1890) by William Morris. They were also instructed that when not reading the book, and still on duty, to have their finger inserted into the book to mark the page they had read up to. The work was an adequate compromise for the missing object – a satchel that belonged to Morris that he carried around for decades, primarily to distribute his manifestos and pamphlets associated with the politics of the Arts and Crafts Movement. This one bag could have been, and most likely was, hugely influential on the political terrain of Britain during the late 1800s. And so, if that bag had not been in those places at those times, British politics and society, as we know it today, might be very different.

Recently I was lucky enough to be invited to a gallery dinner for the opening of the exhibition of a Spanish artist. The work of this particular artist is aggressively political, in fact it is so political it is difficult to appreciate the work on any other level of artistic merit. Ingenious exhibition devices, lightness of materials, intellectuality and the nimbleness of its delivery are all overpowered by the strong, short, certain political messages.

I remember thinking at the time that there was a strange contradiction about the guy who wore a bright yellow puffer jacket emblazoned with a North Face logo, very tight skinny jeans and an effeminate pair of beige suede Ugg boots. The contradiction became all the more apparent as the evening progressed and the drunken artist climbed up onto a table, in the quiet and civilised restaurant, and began shouting the words: "Fuck the power! Fuck the power! Fuck the power! Fuck the power!"

There was a collision I encountered at that moment that I didn't like; an Ugg boot and puffer jacket wearing Marxist? Grimacing with the taste of pseudo politics in the back of my throat, I left the dinner and made my way home. In the back of the cab I drew a small caricature in my notebook to remind me of the night's events. The caricature showed an old bearded man dressed in teenage attire, a speech bubble from his mouth uttering the words: "Fuck the power!" When I looked at the drawing again in the morning, I noticed that magically over his shoulder was slung William Morris' satchel. I was almost certain it was not there the previous night.

A Polaroid photograph documenting the performance 'Assembly' (2009), by Ryan Gander and Jonathan Monk, in which the artists hired actors to play themselves. The actors weren't given any direction. The image shows the two actors mimicking the act of oral sex with one another.

There seems to be a current obsession with collaboration. I was recently given a body warmer that was produced by no fewer than three different entities; Moncler, Junya Watanabe and Comme des Garçons. It's a great body warmer – my autumn, winter and spring staple – and in this case the collaboration probably makes sense. I often find that the relationships between collaborators lack any commonality or purpose though; where the connections between brands becomes a ridiculous PR exercise. Moncler making Rimowa suitcases with interior duvet padding; Hermès producing Leica cameras or helicopter interiors; Porsche producing external hard disk drives; Gucci producing limited edition customised Fiat 500s; Graphic designers designing trainers; artists making fixed-gear bikes; hip-hop stars making art; record producers designing stab vests… All of these examples actually exist. I am all for crossover where there's creative ingenuity, but often it's about making money rather than cultural, or any other, contribution.

Over the years I have collaborated with a number of artists on artworks and projects. My experience is that collaborations between two artists always ends with one doing more of the work or providing more of the creative input than the other. It's just the way it goes; equality is impossible. Perhaps the most interesting collaborative artwork I have made was with Jonathan Monk for the project space of Yvon Lambert, Jonathan's gallery in Paris. The work was called 'Assembly' (2009), which consisted of Jonathan and I going for dinner and drinks together for the evening, whilst we sent two actors (who, it must be said, looked nothing like us nor adopted any of our personal traits) to the gallery opening to play us. Their brief was brief: they were simply told to go to the gallery and stand-in for us and in addition they were given a Polaroid camera and plenty of film to document themselves during the event. When they came to the restaurant to show us the photos and report back they were aggressive and annoyed; they hadn't liked playing us and were insulted we hadn't gone to see it. They threw the Polaroids down onto the table and left. Vaguely surprised by their reactions, Jonathan and I looked through the images, a number of which portrayed us performing acts of fellatio and other minor sexual gratifications on one another. The work wasn't overly successful or particularly well received, but it delivered us both to a place where we'd never been before, to something new, a new understanding (one of my prime objectives in making artworks). The actors understood the true politics of collaboration and made them visible in the Polaroids. Perhaps collaboration is less about working together, instead more a political act of coalition, aligning oneself with allies or individuals of similar interests.

The Polaroids went on sale in the gallery bookshop as a cheap editioned artwork, although the ones that showed Jonathan and I 'at it' were taken out of the pile by Jonathan. I thought they were funny because they were the most telling, so I pocketed them as a storyboard of the evening. They sit pride of place on a shelf in my studio at home.

A4 PAPER[1]

Three boxes of economy 80 g/m^2 A4 printer paper, each box containing five reams, each ream containing five hundred sheets.

There is nothing ostentatious about a sheet of A4 paper. It is a mere practical piece of equipment; solid, standard and serviceable, but in that lies its beauty, for me. The international standard ISO 216 is used by about two thirds of the globe, on first appearance it seems a random, nonsensical scale. A4 measures precisely 210 × 297 mm, though 200 × 300 mm would seem more practical, however the splendour of the A series of paper sizes lies in a mathematical equation. The size is based on a single aspect ratio of the square root of two; meaning that if you fold it in half, its height and width hold the same ratio as before, but the sheet is just smaller.

The confusion caused by the lack of round figures is due, not to notions of width and height, but to the notion of area. A0, the largest of the paper sizes, although measuring 841 × 1189 mm, exactly covers the footprint of one square metre. Its standardisation comes through evolution, a natural selection in design – or in fact – non-design, resulting in ultimate functionality without thought for aesthetic flourish. There is a method in its madness, while on the other hand the history of the American equivalent, known as 'US Letter', lacks sense and beauty. Invented in the early 1980s by Ronald Reagan for American federal forms, the squat, tubby US Letter is a stereotype and a caricature of the American masses from the European viewpoint. It is unwieldy, it lacks motive, and it pines for a history. In relation to true history, 'vintage' pales in comparison.

1. See over leaf

SALE T-SHIRT

A standard large-sized red T-shirt on which 'SALE' is printed in white Helvetica characters, shown alongside a New Era baseball cap in the same colour displaying the phrase 'SOLD OUT'.

I've got a joke for you: fine art course leader meets mother of art student at degree show private view. When introduced to course leader, mother, slightly in awe of what she now realises is a massive infrastructure surrounding her son's mythical pursuit in contemporary art, declares: "Of course I am happy for him, but I don't pretend to understand it". Course leader replies: "Well, Mrs Jones, if he'd have studied quantum physics you wouldn't have pretended to have understood that either!"[1]

I have another joke for you: an artist walks into a bar and orders a pint of beer. During the course of the evening a friend introduces him to a Klingon[2] acquaintance he has not yet met. The first thing the Klingon asks the artist is: "nuq ta' SoH ta'?"[3] The artist pauses, not quite knowing how to reply. During this momentary lapse he considers all the possible answers he could give to such a question. They include: "I work in a bar", "I am a bar tender", "I am between jobs right now" and "I am unemployed". However, the answer he would really like to give is: "I am an artist". After all he regularly attends his studio and does in fact associate the word 'art' with all of the objects that he produces, but because he

1. It wasn't the tutor's answer that makes the story memorable, but the same words coming from the mother's mouth on every occasion after that, attempting to explain her way out of the: "So, what is it he actually does?" question from friends of the family. It became her scapegoat. People aren't intimidated by – or even expected to understand – Stephen Hawking, but unlike the sciences, art belongs to the people, and for the people to take control of it, they must first know it. Fear of the incomprehensible is inescapable.

2. Klingon is a language that was devised by the linguist Dr Marc Okrand in 1982, commissioned by Paramount Pictures for use in the subsequent feature

has never had an exhibition outside the paddings and trappings of his art school degree show, he decides that such an answer would be too pretentious. Besides he is sure that in this particular bar, this would be the most common reply of most of the other patrons. He opts for the: “I work in a bar” reply, courteously followed by: “Why? What do you do?” The Klingon lifts his head smugly and with no humility replies: “nuq taHvIp jIH ’oH tlhIngan vetlh chen Dochmey.”[4] This upsets the artist and he makes a pact with himself that in the future when meeting a new person he shall no longer enquire: “What do you do?” But instead he shall adopt the phrase: “How are you funded?”[5] At that moment an elf walks into the bar and sits down next to the pair. He looks at the Klingon and says: “Malia ten’ yulna?”[6] The Klingon frowns and simply replies: “Sorry, I don’t understand you.”[7]

I have another joke for you: a Klingon finds himself confronted by a display of mannequins in a department store wearing red T-shirts displaying the word ‘sale’ in white, bold, block capitals. The Klingon asks a sales assistant about the possibility of purchasing the garment, but his request is met with nothing more than a smug grin. He is confused, he understands the primary function of a T-shirt is to cover the body, and to provide warmth, protection and humility. He also understands, from his studies of human semiotics, that the T-shirt’s

films of the popular TV series *Star Trek*.

3. “What do you do?”

4. “What fear, I am a Klingon that makes things” (quite sensibly there is no direct translation in the Klingon language for the word ‘pity’, replaced here by the word ‘fear’, and the word ‘art’, replaced here by the word ‘things’).

5. The idea that an artist chooses to call the artist ‘artist’ during a story that’s meant to identify the characteristics that make up an artist is very telling. Your coat is on the hook by the door, leave with your own ideologies.

6. “Care for a drink?”

7. Similarly, the artist communicates in his own idiosyncratic vernacular language – a visual language as complex and subtle as any spoken one. Because the artist developed the language he is in complete control of it. For him it is articulated and pitched to perfection, but that is not to say everyone will understand it. But that’s OK isn’t it?

secondary function is as a vessel for signifiers of personal identity, wealth, and cultural, sociological, and historical background. However the Klingon is confused by the use of the word 'sale' on the T-shirt. Does it mean that the T-shirt is for sale or the hard-shelled, human clone wearing it? Apparently not, the function, it seems, is to announce a reduced-price sale in the shop. So, if the T-shirt was sold and worn would it be interpreted as a signifier of the wearer's irony, wit, ingenuity and creativity in changing the function of the object from an advertising prop to a wearable garment? Or would an onlooker sharing his initial misunderstanding assume that the wearer was for sale? The Klingon frowns, steps back slightly and looks down at his feet in despair, saddened by the fact that this hard-shelled human clone looks nothing like him.

CERAMIC LOVERS' TEAGLASS

A reproduction of Josef and Anni Albers' 'Tea Glass with Saucer and Stirrer' (1925) made by amateur potters attending a ceramics workshop in the Lake District, UK.

In 1925 a recently married young couple called Josef and Anni, working at the Bauhaus in Dessau, Germany, embarked on a collaborative project, which had as much to do with the subject of love as it did with the subject of function dictating form in design. The object they produced was originally a unique prototype tea set, to be photographed and distributed through its documentation, as opposed to being mass-produced (although a few were actually made). It was also a 'pet project', a keepsake, a trophy to mark them finding one another. Their 'Tea Glass with Saucer and Stirrer', nicknamed 'The Lovers' Tea Glass', made from heat-resistant glass, chrome-plated steel, ebony and porcelain, was designed specifically with not one, but two, users in mind. Lovers. With two handles opposite one another, one handle was positioned vertically for the drinker, as you would expect from a tea glass, whilst the opposite handle was positioned horizontally for the maker. The second handle allowed someone to make the tea and pass it to someone else without either burning their fingers. It implied an act of kindness, a gift, a giving, a gesture of affection from one to another. How many times have you made a cup of tea for the person that you love the most and said the words: "Watch your hands, it's hot!"

The thing that seems unimaginable now is the incredulous functionality of their design, which was neither addressed before nor since its production. It's bizarre this design didn't catch on and there are very few original tea glasses by Josef and Anni Albers in existence (most in private or museum collections rather than in use). More poignant however, is the fact that history books describe a very blinkered account of this simple vessel. It is as if the originality and ingenuity of the new, double-function featured in 'The Lovers' Tea Glass' has been forgotten or wiped clean from history. Not only is it difficult to find any description pertaining to the functionality of the dual handled vessel, but also all documentation by private and museum collections portray neither the tea glass being used by two parties, nor its intended functionality by any other method. It usually stands solitary, on a plain, muted, endless surface, with no hands in sight; as if the readers ogling the images should be paying attention to the way it looks as opposed to the reason for its existence. This object that came into being with kindness and love inherent in its form, an object whose form is a direct by-product of its inherent functionality, is portrayed in history merely as an objet d'art.

TINTIN'S OIL DRUM

A reconstructed oil drum from the petrol tanker Speedol Star, which features in *Land of Black Gold* (1972), the fifteenth instalment of the comic strip series *The Adventures of Tintin* by Belgian author and illustrator Hergé.

In my studio there now sits an empty oil drum. Having never seen one in reality before I was amazed at how large it was. Too tall to act as a chair or table, too non-functional to pass for anything else for that matter, it sits like a big space filler waiting to find its place in the world. The key, though, is its back-story; the oil drum is recreated from the petrol tanker, Speedol Star, which features in *Land of Black Gold*[1] a children's story from the series *The Adventures of Tintin*, by Belgian author and illustrator Hergé. It's not real, well, it is real, but its incarnation comes from a fictional reality. The physicalised oil drum is a product of my imagination. One of the true luxuries of an artist's role is that they may conjure into actual being whatever it is they wish to see. This is one object, or prop, from a huge inventory I have produced for a semi-plausible reality; it nestles snugly alongside sculptures, paintings, family photos, mobiles, lamps, furniture, cups, saucers, vehicles, fridge magnets, tools, poems, songs, ringtones, clothing, food and drink, all of which have graced the pages of fiction in one form or another. These objects have been cut from

1. Hergé, *Land of Black Gold*, first published as a comic strip series in Le Petit Vingtième (1939-40) and then in its final, book form by Methuen (1972).

pages, inflated and solidified into physical beings; made real. A quasi-assemblage between this reality and an array of other fictional ones invented by myself and other authors.

My mother enters my studio: "What's the drum for?" I reply: "It's from that ship in the Tintin story, the Speedol Star, do you remember? I had it when I was a kid?" My mother replies: "Not really. How did you get it here?" Frowning, slightly confused by her lack of surprise, I don't really know where to start…

MY FABRIC

A roll of fabric produced by the artist, with a design of the spots and crosses one typically finds on dressmakers' pattern cutting paper. Using this cotton fabric to produce clothing directly makes pattern-cutting obsolete, and the prototype becomes the original.

As a teenager I was taught to cut patterns and sew by my mother, who was a dressmaker and taught home economics as her occupation. I always enjoyed the ability to create something as necessary as clothing, though usually for others (especially my daughter) and occasionally for myself. It occurred to me one day that the process of making one-off clothes with a pattern is wasteful: cutting a sheet of pattern paper to guide fabric cutting and then discarding it. There are also too many stages to a dressmaking process: selecting the pattern and size, cutting out the paper pattern, pinning the paper to the fabric, cutting the fabric out and unpinning the paper ready to begin. Those five steps alone take place before so much as picking up a needle or looking at a sewing machine.

Dressmakers and tailors who produce their own patterns use a paper, thicker than a standard pattern paper, with a texture and weight similar to sugar paper. It is printed with a pattern of dots and crosses in pale blue ink, the idea being that they can draw freehand or trace around other components of clothing or patterns, using the dots and crosses as guides and markers. Tailors use a specific chalk, a flattened triangular disc, that can be magically dusted away from the fabric no matter how hard the tailor draws with it. On many occasions I have witnessed the moment after the markings have been made on clothing in production or during alteration, but before it has been cleaned. A garment covered in crosses, dashes, darts, arrows and lines, telling the story of its production is a great looking thing.

A few years ago all these things mixed in my mind and I produced a cotton fabric pre-printed with the dots and crosses of dressmaker and tailor's pattern cutting paper. You can draw directly on the fabric, cut from it and produce a unique final garment, which then acts as a vessel for the story of how it was made. The device means a prototype is elevated to the status of an original, undermining the mass-produced nature of most clothes. The aesthetics of the fabric incidentally become inherited from its function, as opposed to being hereditary of its form.

ALBERS' 'FIREPLACE' BRICKS AND FRENCH ROOF TILES

A pallet of Vitcas fire bricks made from dense clay, each brick measuring 230 × 114 × 76 mm, produced to withstand temperatures up to 1300°C, for domestic applications including fireplaces, stoves and furnaces. Shown alongside a pile of handmade roofing tiles reclaimed from a rural stone farmhouse in the Cahors region of Southern France.

I've had the idea 'mould for multifunctional brick' scrawled in my notebooks for years, transferred from one to another when the various unrealised projects have been reviewed and reinvigorated, copied into lists in the backs of new journals. The idea was first written when I saw an image of Josef Albers' 'Fireplace' (1955), built in off-white firebricks, for the Irving Rowe House, North Haven, USA. The fireplace prompted me to attempt to rethink the idea of a brick, well, a mould for a brick, as a single brick is of little use after all. The idea is not to make a 'material', but a 'tool' to enable the production of materials – to enable communities to build freely. The idea is for the brick to be solid on its X and Y axes but hollow on its Z axis, allowing it to be used to create solid walls, as well as windows and chimney flues. The idea is to make a mould that can be used extensively without deterioration and that can be used to make inexpensive bricks from easily sourced materials (clay, cement and earth for example), which would be especially useful in developing countries. Furthermore, its ability to produce entire walls that are structurally solid yet entirely open would benefit communities in countries with hot climates. Its versatility could be extended if the mould was used with lightweight materials, such as shredded paper with a PVA glue fixative, allowing the user to create indoor seating, shelving and work surfaces. Perhaps this is the year for the idea to fall from the pages of my notebook into reality.

There's a roof tile, so geographically significant to the south of an exacting line in rural France, that it's said historians can identify building locations in old photographs from the shape of the tiles alone. In 2004 my wife and I were holidaying in the Cahors region of Southern France, staying in a small, medieval stone house that had been rebuilt by hand using original tools and techniques by the Flemish owner, Chris Bert. He'd sold his Michelin starred restaurant in Antwerp to buy an area of land on which lay a medieval village in ruins. Over a ten year period he'd managed to single-handedly rebuild six of the 20 or so buildings, working mainly in the spring and autumn, whilst relaxing in the summer heat (and tending to the tourists, like ourselves, who stayed in the buildings which he had restored), and moving to warmer climates to stay with friends during the bleak winters.

I watched him riding around his land on golf carts, shooting wild boar and foraging for truffles with his ferocious dog, as well as spending time drinking and storytelling with him, and his wife Sidonie, until late into the evenings. I also picked up some knowledge on the subject of medieval architecture and building methods. Many of Chris' house roof tiles he had found buried intact under piles of earth on his land. Originally made by hand from a terracotta clay-like substance, the tiles were not made by the hand of the builder, but by the hand of the matriarchal family figure. French roof tiles in rural Southern France were produced during the summer by the mother, sitting outside the kitchen door with a great pile of clay, she would take a lump and shape it over her thigh. The beauty and efficiency of the tiles lay in the tapered shapes of the thighs of the well-fed women moulding them. This tapering allowed the roof tiles to tessellate, one overlapping another, forming a weatherproof membrane over the roof of the building.

I remember Chris joked that the builder with the fattest wife was the luckiest because he'd have the largest tiles, requiring fewer tiles to cover the roof and less time fitting the tiles. Although Chris was joking there was logic to the idea and a beauty in its economy of means. Throughout history, in rural France, it was a measure of status to have an overweight wife, the implication being that the family was well fed on rich, fatty foods, which meant they had the wealth to obtain them. There have been many signs of status throughout history that contradict our contemporary signifiers of affluence and social stratification: in Victorian England, young women were considered more attractive and affluent the lighter their skin colour (which resulted in many women chalking their skin and even their hair to gain a whiter complexion). The more pale the complexion, the more time spent inside at leisure – embroidering, arranging flowers, learning the harp etc. – rather than working outside in the fields exposed to the sun, which browned the skin. More often nowadays, suntanned skin is an indication of the wealth associated with holidaying in exotic places, whilst a pale complexion suggests working endlessly indoors in a shop, factory or office; going to work before the sun rises and going home after the sun sets.

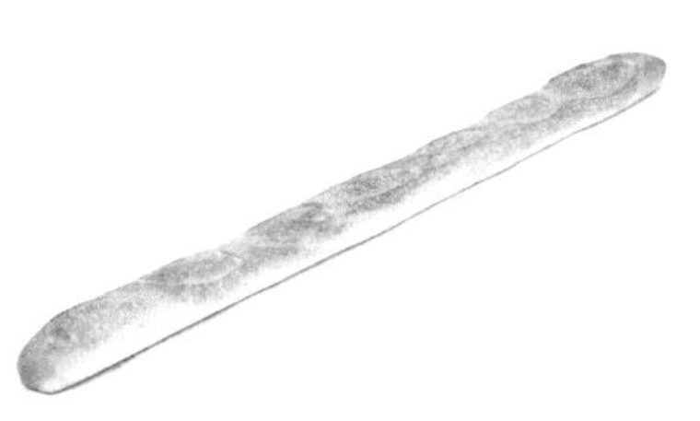

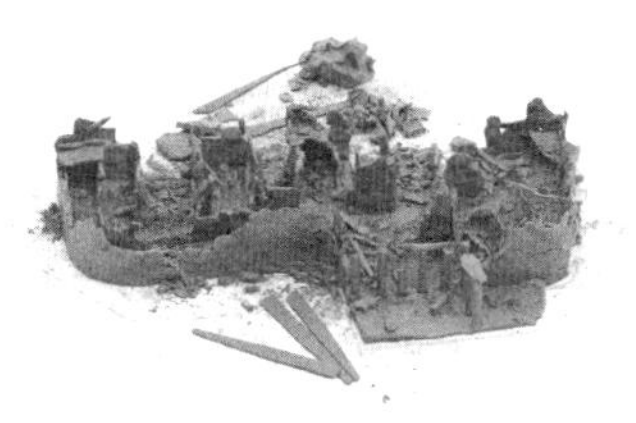

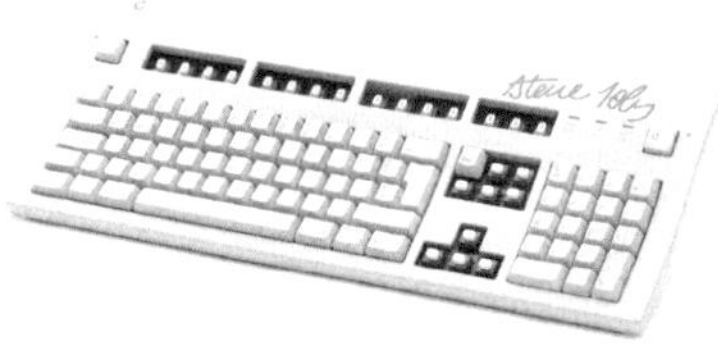

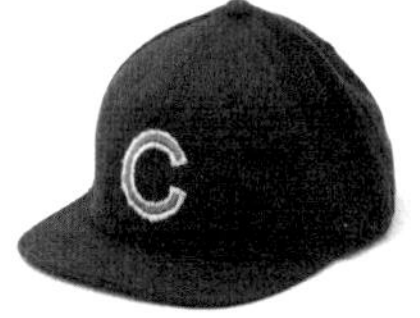

p. 11 p. 12

p. 14 p. 15

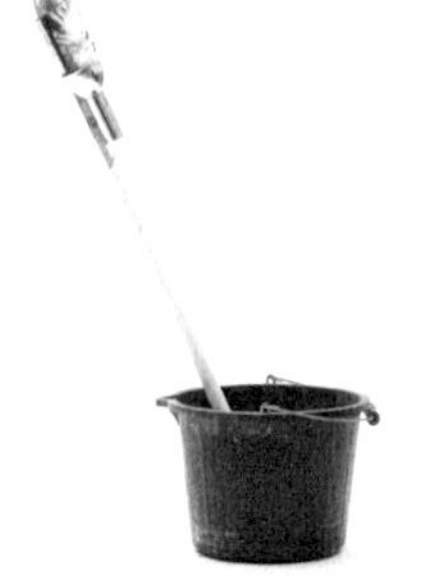

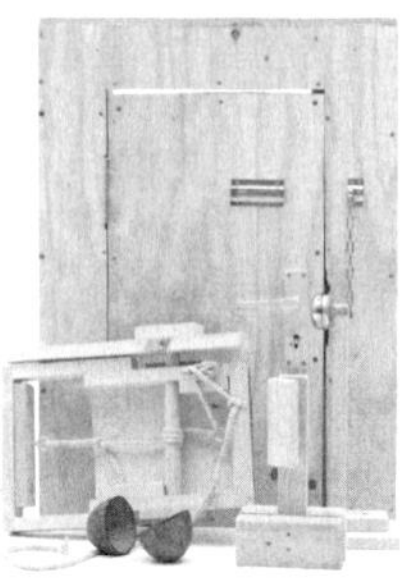

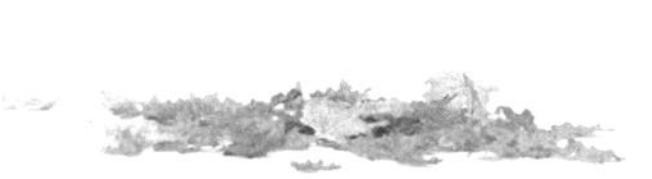

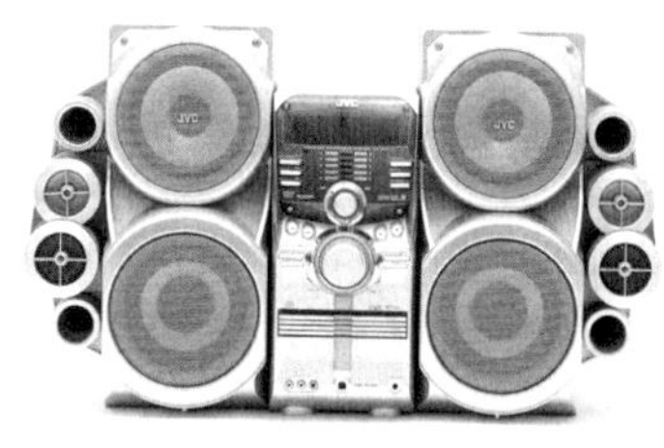

p. 17 p. 19

p. 20 p. 23

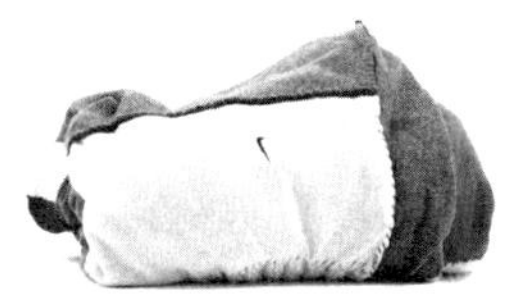

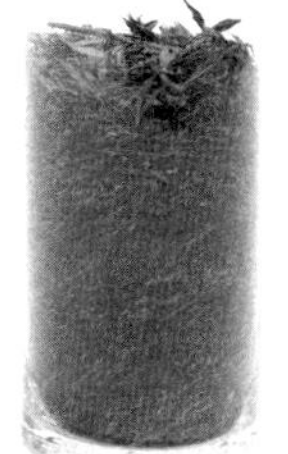

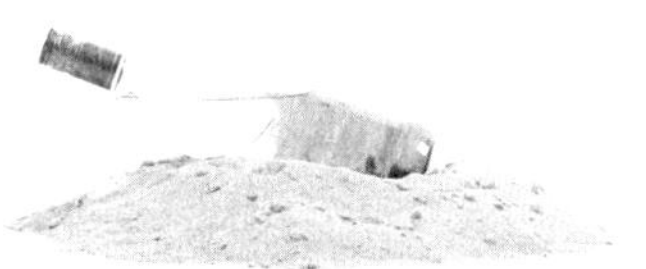

p. 25 p. 27

p. 46 p. 50

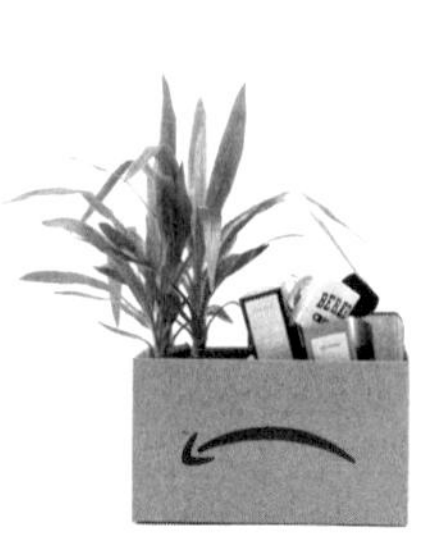

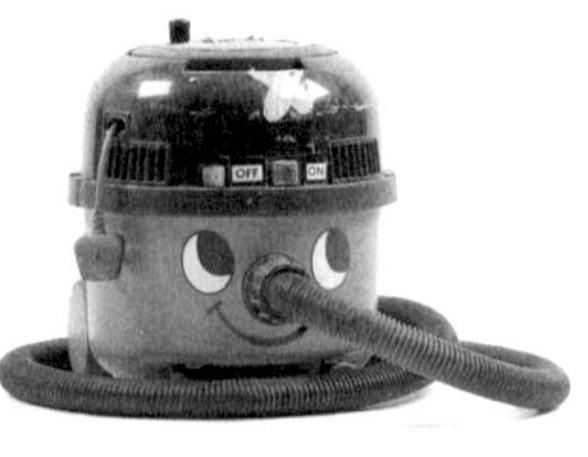

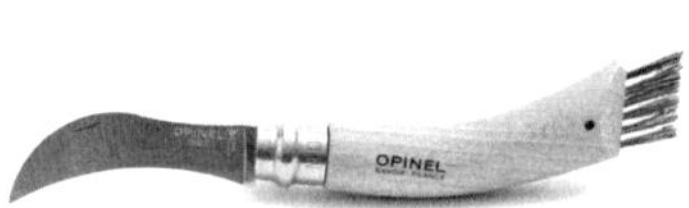

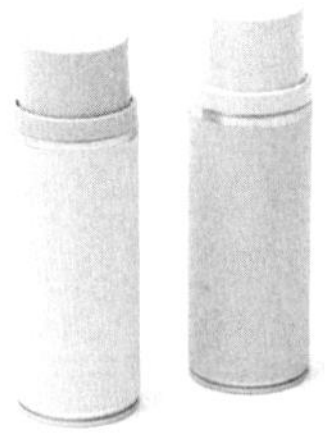

p. 52 p. 54

p. 58 p. 63

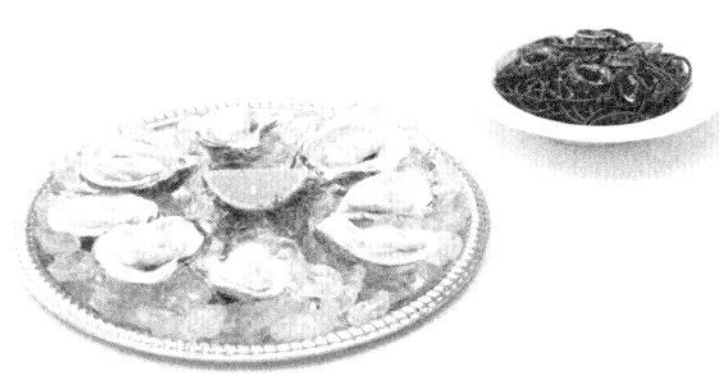

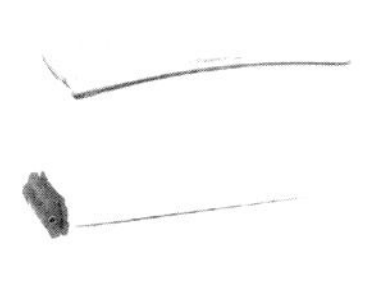

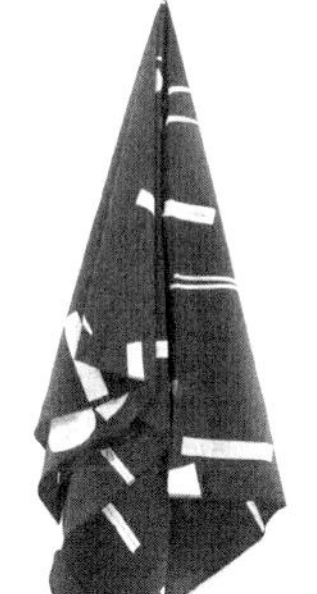

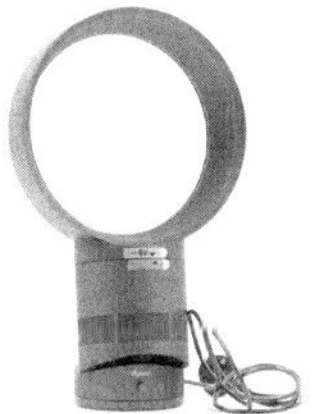

p. 65 p. 70

p. 73 p. 76

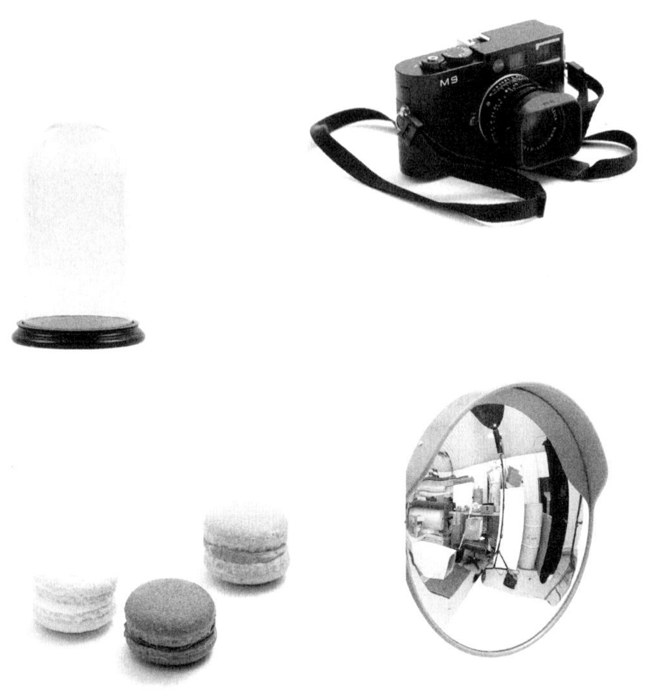

p. 80 p. 83

p. 86 p. 89

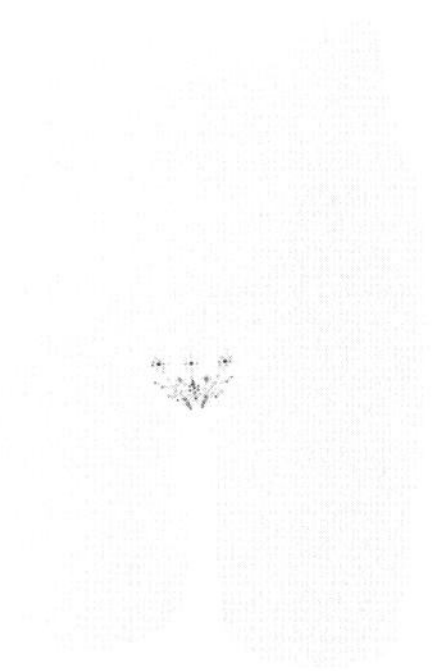

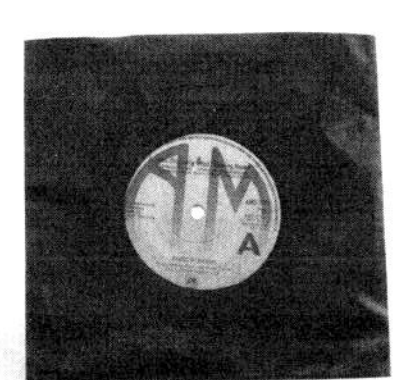

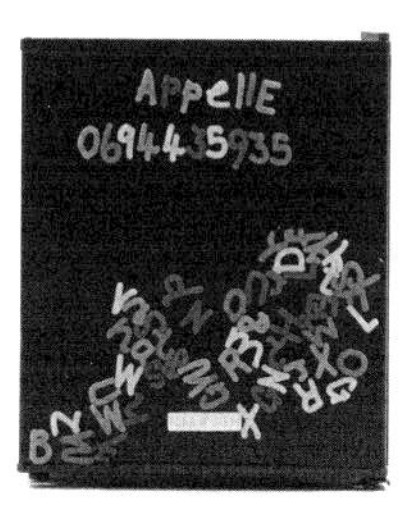

p. 91 p. 94

p. 96 p. 101

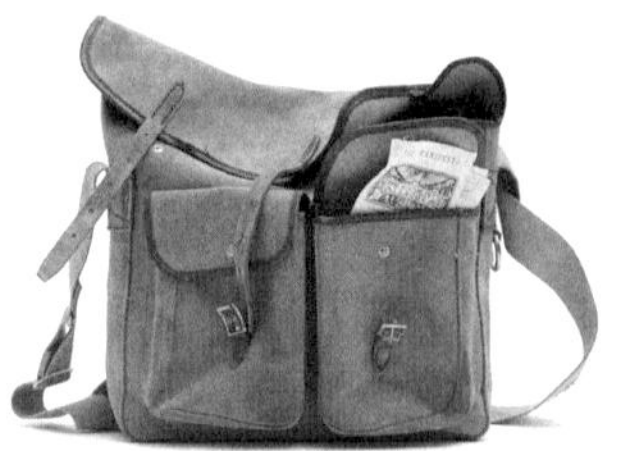

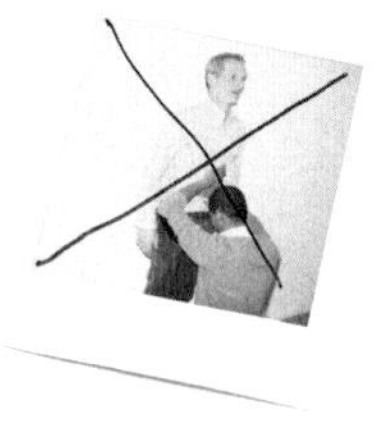

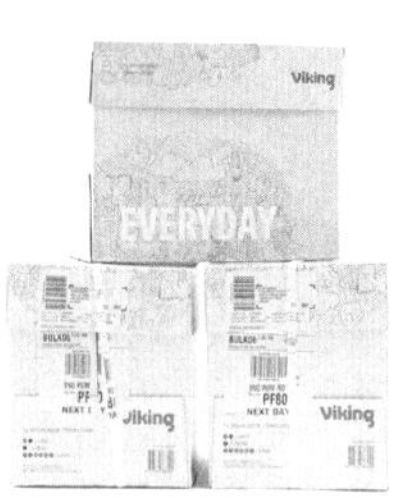

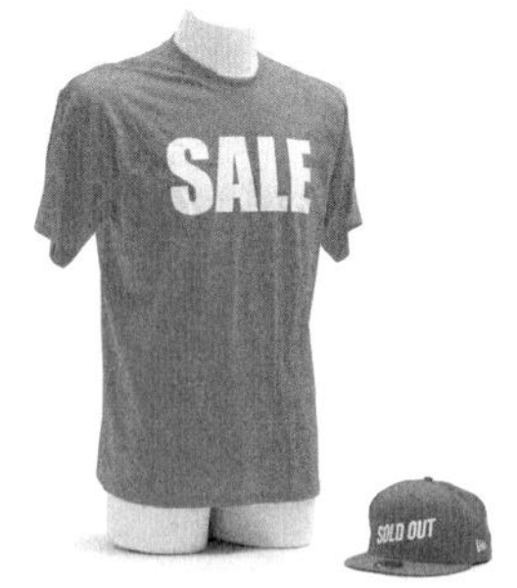

p. 106 p. 109

p. 112 p. 116

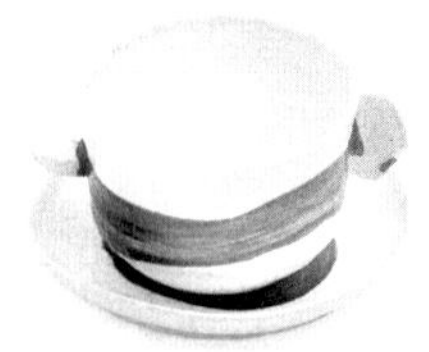

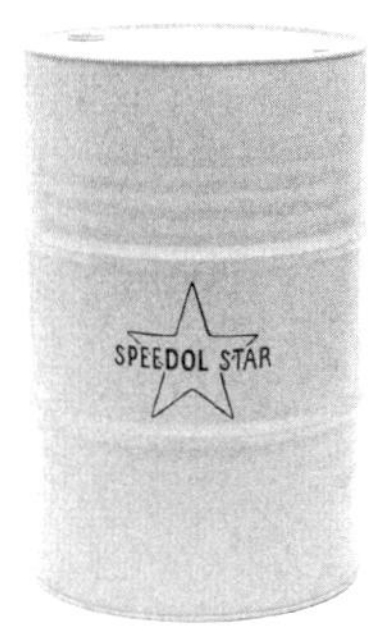

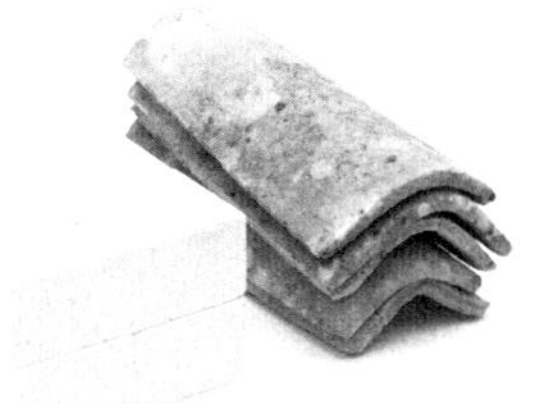

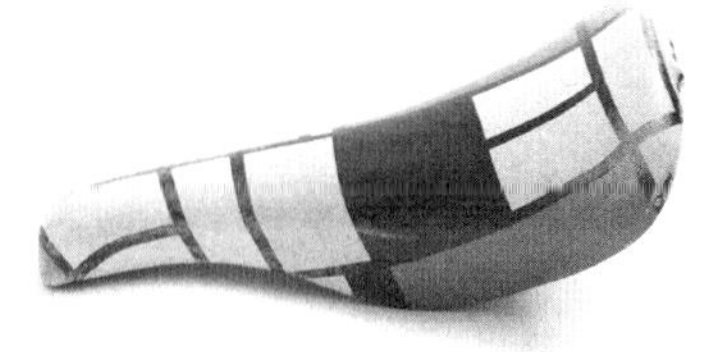

p. 119 p. 121

p. 123 p. 125

p. 129

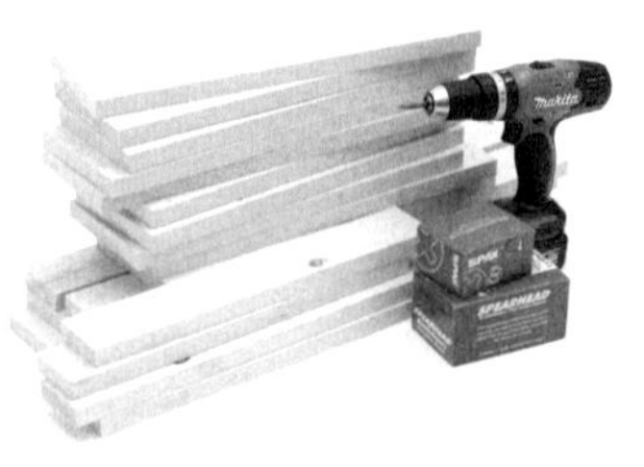

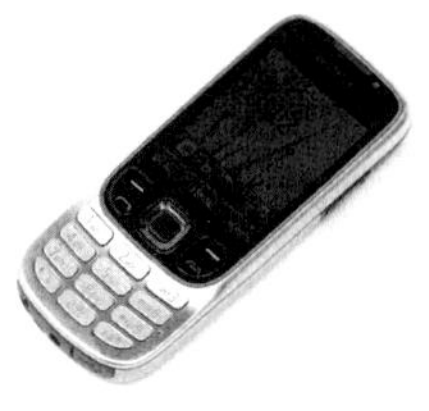

BEST DAD

BEST DAD

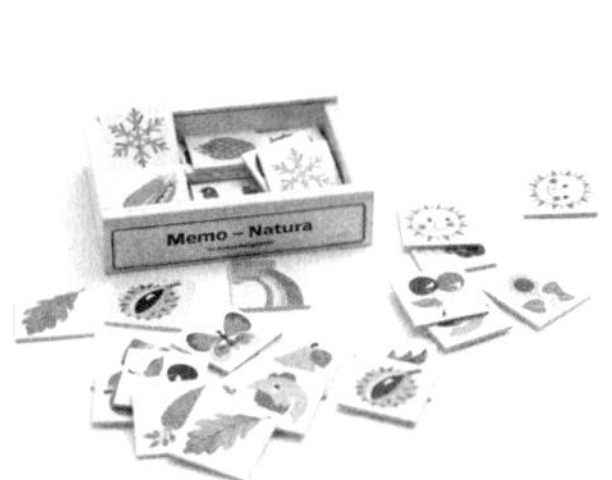

p. 132 p. 151

p. 153 p. 156

p. 160

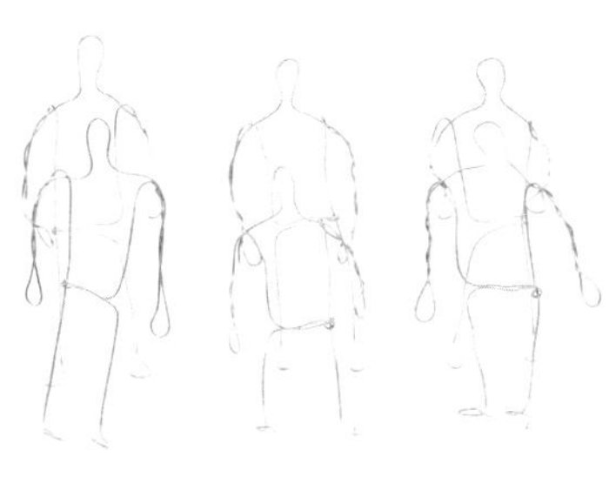

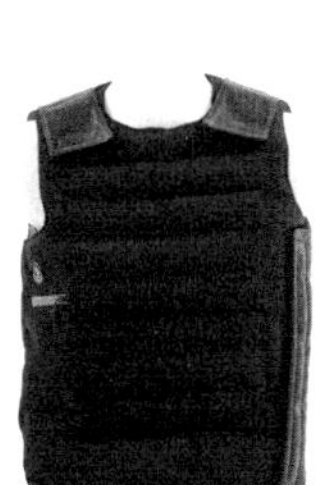

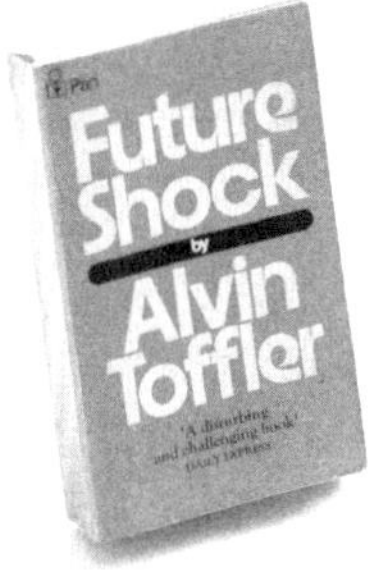

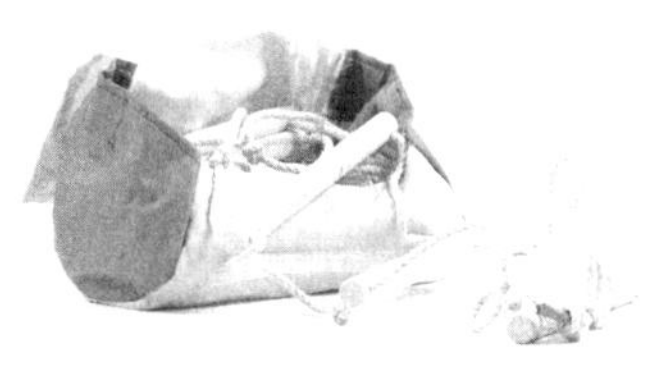

p. 162 p. 165

p. 167 p. 168

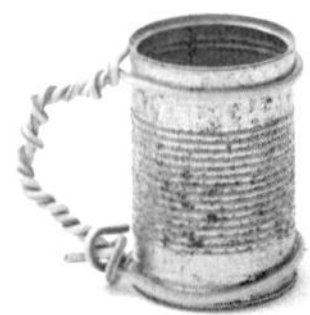

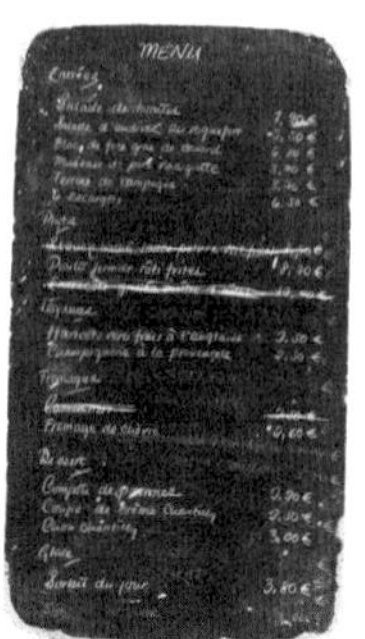

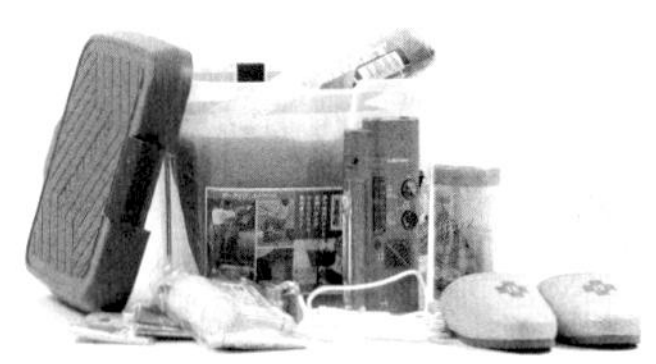

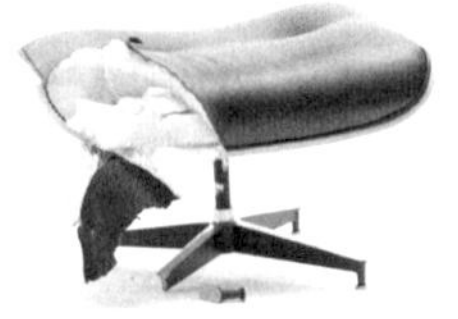

p. 170 p. 173

p. 175 p. 178

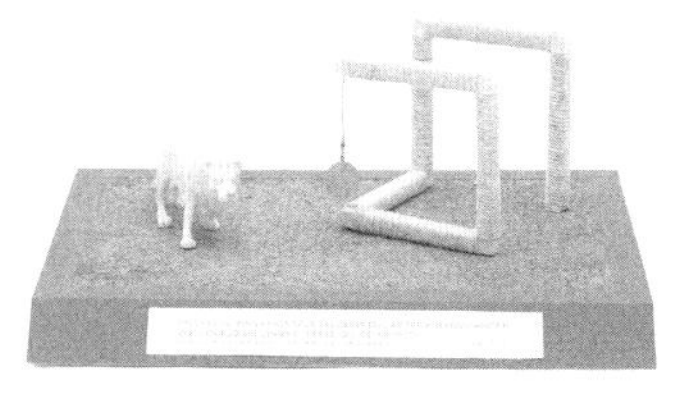

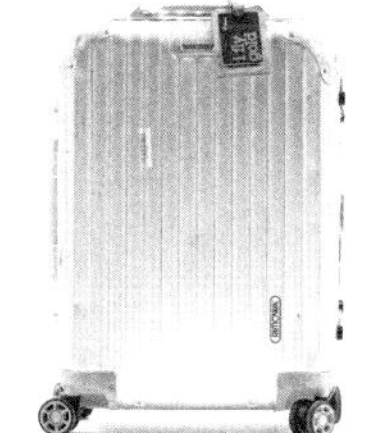

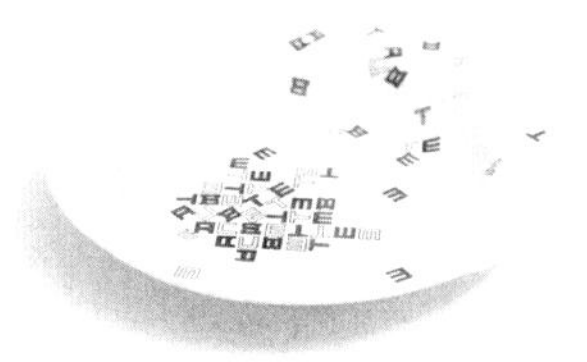

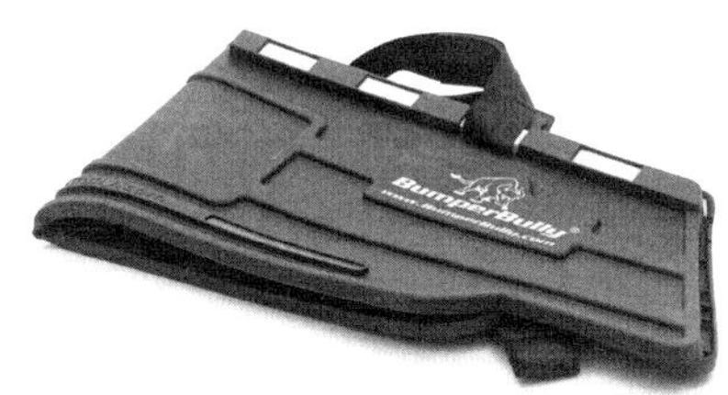

p. 181 p. 183

p. 185 p. 187

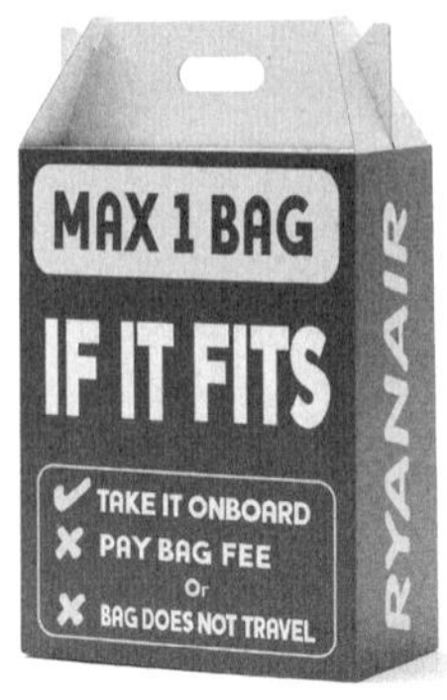

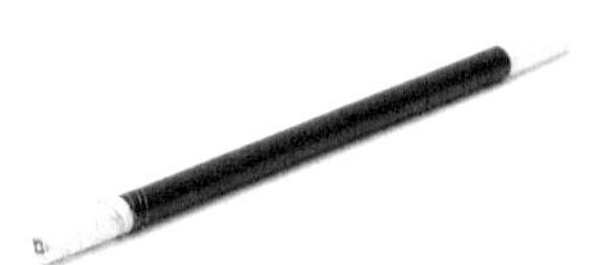

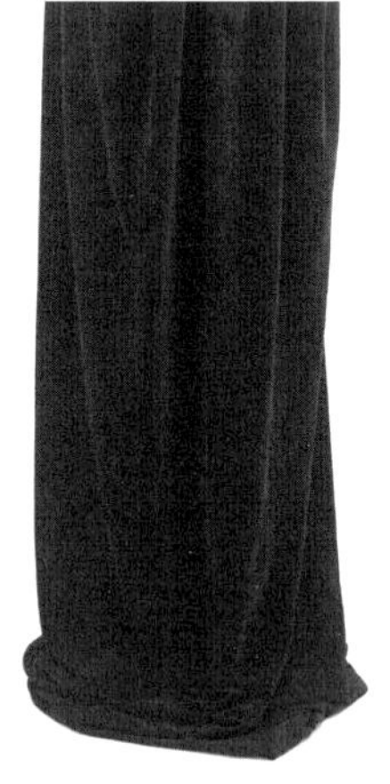

p. 188 p. 193

p. 196

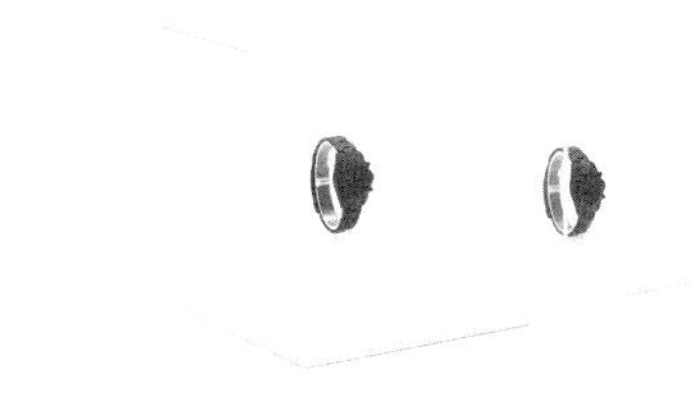

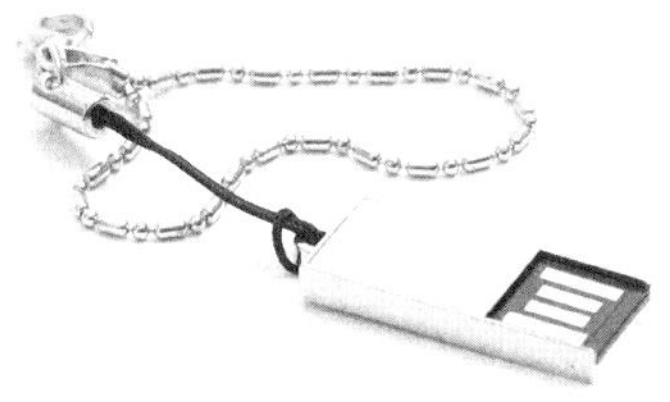

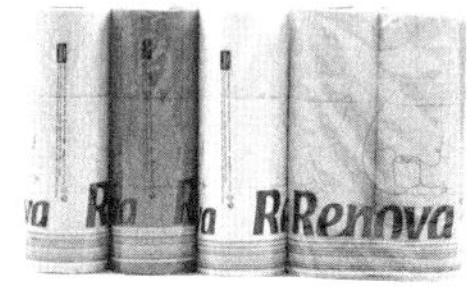

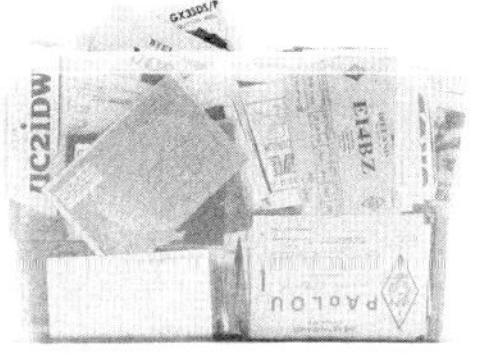

p. 197 p. 198

p. 203 p. 205

p. 210

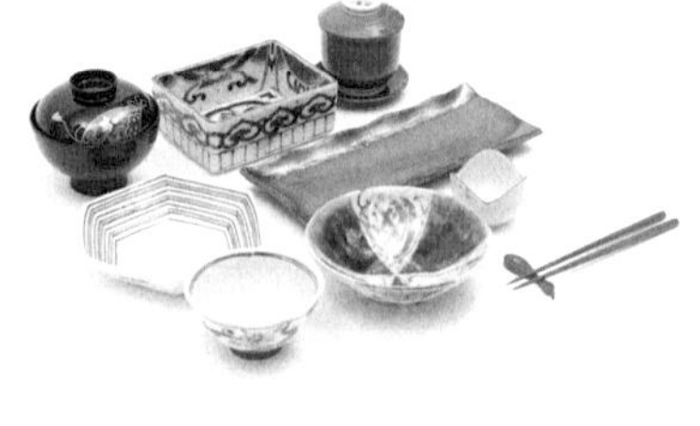

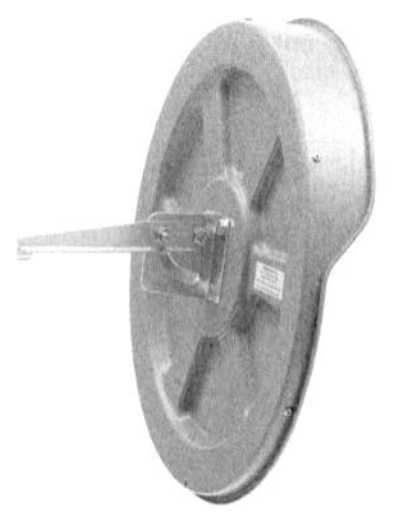

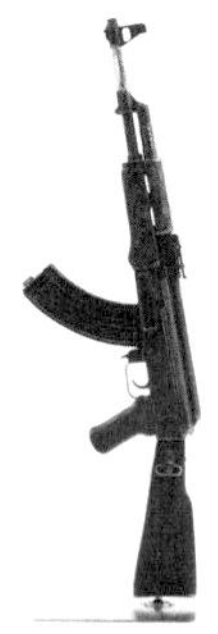

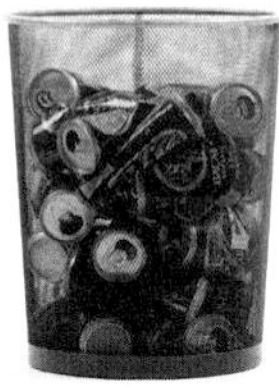

p. 213 p. 216

p. 217 p. 219

SADDLE

A commercially available cycling saddle decorated with a Mondrian-esque pattern produced by the French ski and bicycle equipment manufacturer LOOK, and similar to one used by the artist's brother Neil as a teenager.

'Counter Composition XV' (1925), a composition that is counter to what? That's what I remember thinking as an art student leafing through the pages of a book on Theo van Doesburg. At the time, I was in awe of these paintings and wished I had made them. I had no ideas of my own; I didn't understand art's capacity to change the way we think about the world. I just wanted to be an artist. I just wanted to be van Doesburg. About ten years later, when I began to read the texts in art catalogues (as opposed to just looking at the pictures) I worked out what exactly these compositions were counter to. Van Doesburg's composition was counter to Piet Mondrian's. The story goes that Mondrian and van Doesburg became good friends. They established the art movement De Stijl together. But when van Doesburg moved to Paris with his wife Nelly in 1923, the two artists saw more of each other and they began to bicker over their differing ideologies. The following year Mondrian and van Doesburg had an almighty row, said to have been over the 'dynamic aspect of the diagonal line'. Subsequently, they fell out and never spoke again, but such rigidity and rigour surrounded their individual beliefs on the simplicity of turning a canvas 45°, that a corner of art history was changed forever. Mondrian's geometric compositions aesthetically peppered my childhood and teenage years. His images were endlessly reproduced and encountered. A signature style that became an emblem for modern art. A Mondrian is in fact now, in many imaginations, an illustration of art, a motif of itself. The first time I remember seeing this was in the early 1980s while watching televised footage of the Tour de France with my brother Neil, an avid road racer. The cycling team La Vie Claire sported clothing with a Mondrian-inspired motif, and rode bicycles with designs derived from Mondrian's patterns. The image of my brother's Mondrian saddle cover will always remain burned into my memory. And since then I have noticed the style elsewhere: Mondrian's patterns have fallen into the pages of the Miffy books, Dutch children's stories about a cartoon rabbit; adorned the sides of central heating installation vans; and wrapped themselves around aerosol canisters of hairspray.

Of course, I am talking about Mondrian, not his counter composition competition. However, for me, it is van Doesburg who wins. You see Van Doesburg quotes Mondrian, while shrugging off his preoccupation with practice, development and work ethic. The black lines of 'Counter Composition XV' are beefed up, rendered in bold, and, it seems to me, its 45° twist holds no aesthetic reasoning. It is to deliver exactly that, a twist, an altered perspective, but maybe more importantly, by that fact that we know it is askew, we also know that it is not a Mondrian, yet manages to mutter everything Mondrian says under its breath. Read from my perspective, this work has more in common with a piece of conceptual art made today than a Neo-Plasticism painting from more than 80 years ago. It is cocky, light on its feet, considered. It understands its history, its legacy and its position in the world. It has balls and it contains a multitude of qualities that I, as a practicing conceptual artist today, consider ingredients for a kick-ass work of art. When I think about the diagonal feud between Mondrian and van Doesburg, it strikes me that such a closed-down mentality and stubbornness would be impossible to maintain today. I'm reminded of something an artist friend from Glasgow called Michael Fullerton once told me. He explained that Glasgow is an easier place to make artwork than London, because you spend your evenings in Glasgow drinking with another artist, someone you want to make better work than. Maybe having some opposition is a good place to start, a watershed of some kind, or a counter competition. After all, is it not difference of opinion that keeps us current?

The components and tools required to produce a Crate Chair designed by Gerrit Rietveld in 1934.

An entrance hall, Maastricht, The Netherlands, September 1999

On arriving in The Netherlands in 1999 for postgraduate study I was greeted in the entrance space of the Jan van Eyck Academie by a huddle of chairs and tables made from untreated sawn timber. The area where these chairs congregated was used as a meeting place for participants. Bread would be broken, stories would be told, friends would be made and sexually transmitted diseases would be shared...

Quite unwittingly, this huddle of furniture became part of my life. It transpired that the chairs were made by a burly Dutch man called Huub, the technical advisor of the Academie's woodwork shop. Meanwhile, the bogus red cotton-covered foam blocks that acted as cushions – and which seemed to bastardise the principles of the chairs' obviously modernist design – were made by the Academie's secretary at home on her sewing machine. I grew fond of Huub during my stay there. He wasn't the most approachable of people, and many of my fellow participants found him really hard to work with. Thinking back now that might have had something to do with his hard, working-class work-ethic. I guess if you take someone from industry, as he was, and drop them in an over-funded art school with a pack of trans-global spoilt brats walking around with laptops and wearing designer specs, there's bound to be a bit of friction. I got to know Huub through my interest in his Rietveld furniture. I found out he'd once had a mini production line making these tables and chairs, about fifteen years beforehand when he was first employed by the Academie. Fifty-five chairs and twenty side-tables to be exact. Pinned to the wall of his windowless box-room office at the back of the workshop were a few black and white A3 photocopies of a very dated-looking plan for the furniture. We would sit there together, drinking coffee and talking about these plans, which he assured me were very rare, although he would never tell me how he came upon them. The day I left Maastricht to go and live in Amsterdam, I found an envelope pushed under the door of the bare studio I was about to leave which contained photocopies of the plans and a Post-it note which read: "Don't show anyone", stuck to the first page. Two weeks later, by chance, I came across a newly-published book entitled *Rietveld Meubels om Zelf te Maken/How to Construct Rietveld furniture* (2008) in the shop of the Stedelijk Museum with exactly the same plans in it. I soon discovered that the photocopies Huub had so preciously given me were from the 1986 second edition of that book. I initially felt a little deflated, but in retrospect I think Huub was trying to instil in my mind, or preserve in his own, some kind of uniqueness or exclusivity around the chairs to curb their increasing popularity. At this point, however, the significance of that furniture for me had not quite yet been realised.

Utrecht, The Netherlands, May 1936

Gerrit Rietveld was born in Utrecht and stayed there all his life. His father was a cabinetmaker and Gerrit started working in his shop at the age of twelve. By 1934 he was a qualified architect and making a lot of furniture. That year he designed a series of utilitarian furniture intended for the masses, produced by Metz & Co. of Amsterdam. This was during the depression, and the furniture was designed in direct response to the harsh economic climate of the early '30s. The pieces were made from cheap, red spruce usually used for packing cases, and designed for self-assembly at home. The series was called 'Crate Furniture'. Being prone to exaggeration and embellishment, when relating this story I often tell people that the lengths of sawn timber are cut without waste from the exact dimensions of planks taken from cargo crates containing tea from the Dutch colony of Surinam. Who knows? ...No, really, I mean, who knows? I would love to hear this story confirmed.

Rietveld proposed:

> *...a piece of furniture made of high-grade wood and manufactured completely according to traditional production methods is transported in a crate to avoid damage... no one has ever ascertained that such a chest embodies an improvised, highly purposeful method of carpentry... there must therefore at long last be someone who chooses the crate rather than the piece of furniture.*[1]

1. Peter Drijver and Johann Niemeijer, *Rietveld Meubels om Zelf te Maken/How to Construct Rietveld furniture*, Thoth Uitgeverij, 2008.

Unfortunately, I don't think the idea ever really quite caught on. Certainly the chairs weren't very popular at the time.

An artist's studio, London, UK, November 2005

Fred Evans, aged six, accompanied by his mother Caroline, is invited to my studio, given twenty planks of sawn timber, the materials of a deconstructed Rietveld 'Crate Chair', and told to make something. Fred strategically, or perhaps randomly, selects two pieces and positions them butted up against each other at a jaunty angle. I drill a hole, countersink and insert a screw to join pieces together for him. This process continues until all the pieces are used. This is an experiment that I have thought about doing for quite some time without really knowing why. Throughout Fred's work I am encouraging, but consciously attempting to censor myself from contributing creatively to the construction process. I realise later that I wasn't really censoring myself enough, but enough for what? It isn't an experiment because I don't have a hypothesis to prove or disprove, or any research methods from which to document results and draw conclusions. I remember this from GSCE science lessons. I also remember that one of the most important things in an experiment is the Control. To achieve reliable findings the conditions of the experiment must be identical each time the experiment is conducted. I find myself toying with the idea of repeating this exercise, ten times, to make the process more scientific. The thesis seems to be developing backwards. I note to myself that nothing must change apart from the subject – which I realise is the child, not the chair.

In truth, Fred Evans, aged six, accompanied by his mother Caroline, paid two visits to my studio. The first was not too dissimilar to the way I described it previously, but there are notable discrepancies. Fred actually began to assemble the pieces given to him in a very ordered and considered manner. At some point during the process, to my horror the object he was making started to resemble a box, and slowly as time passed, as piece by piece was added, it became apparent that he was, in fact, the son of Sol LeWitt. He was making a perfect cube, the little bastard! That cube was undoubtedly the most flawless part of the whole project, but obviously I wasn't after flawlessness. At this point I felt that the experiment hadn't really yet begun and the conditions weren't exactly in place. As it happened, Fred started to get a little aggravated too, perhaps partly brought on by the sugar in the tube of Smarties and Lemonade I had on offer. The object he was making didn't have the jaunty angles and protruding struts I had expected from a 6 year-old let loose with these materials, and although I feel quite bad about it now, I had the idea that both Fred and his mum Caroline could sense my bewilderment and surprise, which they may have confused with disappointment, which led to the decision by all parties involved that the partially-constructed sculpture should be disassembled and the process recommenced afresh the following week. I feel quite accountable for this. If Fred had been left to his own devices we would probably be looking at an interesting anomaly rather than the pleasingly abstract contraption that was produced by him on his following visit. My guilt is bubbling away here. Still… one-nil to me.

A kitchen table, London, UK, June 2006

I spent a bit of time thinking about the 'Faux-Modernist' thing some more after Stuart yelled at me and told me I really should get my story straight before writing anything down. And I came up with this: There's a lot of art and design around at the moment that uses an appropriated modernist aesthetic. Traditionally, we think of the modernist aesthetic as borne from ethics, or at least an explicit set of values, function above form, etc. So how does that translate into the idea of an artwork that exudes these values but is not necessarily produced under them? This work surely becomes purely emblematic; something that visually or iconically reminds us of a set of values because it looks like another thing originally made by that yardstick. There is an obvious difference between simply referencing modernist form – keying into a history – and actually working under its values, and I guess I was getting upset about the ubiquity of the former. But what about my non-experiment? There's indeed part of me that wants to make a 'modernist-looking' sculpture which is 'easy' (both physically and aesthetically). And I'm sure I could make a really convincing one and I'd really enjoy making it. But it's problematic. Since the mid '90s that modernist look is an easy art world currency that I increasingly find myself criticising, like in the pub. In effect I'm cancelling myself out of the possibility of doing it myself, or at the very least setting myself up for a bout of self-loathing, which I can do without. I realise, then, that asking Fred to assist me in this process is actually some subconscious counter-process I'm setting up to achieve a clone of what I wish to critique – or maybe highlight is a better word – without actually making it myself, but still enjoying the creation. Making it one step removed, then, and conceptually it works like child's play. My undercover idea was that all the sculptures made by the children would appear – to any spectator unaware of the conditions under which they had been made – to be a generic sculpture made by an artist now, at this time, in this city, London, in this epoch, that will come to be known in the future as the era of 'Faux-Modernism'. I want to be part of it so as not to be part of it. My hypothesis had formed. I will make ten sculptures with ten children, each from a single deconstructed Rietveld 'Crate Chair'. I expect that the majority will be functionless, abstract, chaotic forms reminiscent of a stereotypical constructivist or modernist aesthetic. There are two important points to consider: one, the makers have no knowledge of modernist ethics, values and principles; and two, the material (wood) previously constituted modernist ethics, values and principles. If the hypothesis was proved correct, I decided, it would be for one of these two reasons: one, children are inherently inclined to make something that approximates the modernist aesthetics described previously, i.e., their naivety matches that of modernism; or two, the essence or spirit of modernism is transferred through materials, i.e., has somehow got into the wood. I hadn't (and haven't) yet worked out how to divide the two. That's for a later experiment. Anyway, with this hypothesis in mind I decide to make nine more sculptures under the same conditions.

An artist's studio, London, UK, February 2006

I'm being advised by Rose, the younger sister of my girlfriend. It's the first time I've met her, and I'm a bit distracted from the work in hand because of the significance of the social situation. When it's over, we're off to the Hard Rock Café on Park Lane for a burger and a milkshake, followed by a drive to the Suffolk countryside to take Rose home. You might say I'm seeing things through Rose-tinted spectacles. In fact, the making of this sculpture has pretty much escaped my memory, but looking back at the pictures, it seemed to be a hybrid of order and chaos, a sort of systematic muddle. The object was made in two halves, I remember that. The first section was a cross laid on the floor, and I think we talked about it being a bit like a canal system, and the second section, which we later joined to the first part, was more like an incomplete cube. I do remember a sheet of holographic acid-house smiley stickers were on a table in my studio for some reason, and I passed them to Rose to see if she wanted them. Rose stuck one onto the sculpture to brand it. I remember thinking that I'd ruined the experiment again, because I'd not stuck to the control conditions. Shortly after, I also wondered if I should've been using the word 'sculpture' when talking with her about it. After all doesn't 'sculpture' already suggest something abstract or alien-looking? Something non-functional, decorative, which again messes up the supposedly neutral conditions.

A gallery, Amsterdam, The Netherlands, June 2006

I am working in the gallery with my gallerist's son, Abel, on a sculpture which will be exhibited in the show as soon as it is made and he knows it. He is seven years old. He is an extraordinary child, in fact there's something prodigal about him. He is by far the most coy and hesitant of all the kids, but also the most astute, and he works very, very fast. The thing he makes does, actually, in all honesty, look very much like 'Tatlin's Tower', yet built in the most illogical way. For a start he builds it lying down, and only right at the end stands it up. He explains to me where the cars should park underneath, and how the lifts go up and down the sides and where people can enter and exit. It isn't at all abstract to him, but it's not logical or considered either. Although it immediately appears abstract to a stranger, he has obviously made clear sense of the abstraction. It is the most beautiful so far, by quite some way, though I still can't really fathom why. Perhaps it's something to do with the fact that while it appears abstract, there's a certain familiarity to the angles, mass, line, form and weight, so it's not uncomfortably spastic. Its form lies well within the psyche, but very latent and subconscious. This suddenly seems somewhere beyond that simple emblem referencing modernist history. At this point I feel I might actually be learning something.

A gallery, Bologna, Italy, April 2006

In Italy I'm making a Rietveld reconstruction with Diego, the grandson of the caretaker of the pavilion where the show is. We are working in the living space of Le Corbusier's Esprit Nouveau Pavilion, presented to the City of Bologna by the City of Paris. The original building was realised as an ephemeral pavilion for the Paris Universal Expo in 1925 and rebuilt more than fifty years later in 1977 in the middle of Bologna Fair District. Diego is given the parts that would usually make up two chairs and one side table. Again, not exactly under the precise conditions I spoke about before, I know, but I'm caring less and less about the control. The energy and excitement I get from the act of making these sculptures is increasingly substituting any need for analytical results. My subject this time is a boisterous Italian 9 year-old who naturally doesn't speak any English. The sculpture is made with the help of a translator. He quickly gets to work and, again, to my surprise, constructs a gigantic tower, constructed in three separate parts that I am directed to stack one on top of the other and fix together. The idea that this is assembled from three separate components is an oddity, but I'm intrigued. I can't help but think that somehow he was aware of the fact that the singular pile of wooden planks he was given was derived from three separate entities. The outcome is therefore in line with my materials theory.

An art fair, London, UK, October 2006

This situation feels like a pressure cooker. It's the opening of the Frieze Art Fair in London, and what started as a simple exercise has unnecessarily evolved into a spectacle. There is a large audience, as well as sundry photographers and a BBC film crew. In addition, it turns out that Santa's little helper this time is not one child, but two. I feel very awkward and uncomfortable in this situation, and begin to question whether I am making these poor kids perform like dancing bears. I certainly feel like I'm dancing myself. To ease the situation I suggest to the kids' mother that the work should be carried out by just one of the sisters, rather than both of them – namely the eldest, again called Rose. This is translated into Dutch to the two girls standing patiently in front of the pile of wood. Word by word I witness the youngest girl's face slowly drop from a beaming smile to one of disappointment. Then I see her eyes well up with tears, and she starts blinking fast so as not to cry, in an attempt to be grown-up for the crowd. A minute later she is bawling uncontrollably in her mother's arms. I feel like the audience are all looking at me, frowning and tutting, accompanied by mutterings from the crowd: "Oh why doesn't he make it with them both?" "Poor kid, she really wanted to do it…" I feel like a bad guy. It's terrible, so I rapidly go back on my decision and hold out a piece of wood at arms length, beckoning the youngest to join in, and they're soon both at work. It's by far the quickest sculpture to date due to the gruelling situation. The result is as anticipated this time: a beautiful monster.

An artist's studio, London, UK, March 2006

At this point I had a new idea. I realised it was a bit late into the process to be changing things, but I had recently found eight bags of second-hand books at my local library on Camomile Street and I made the decision to add one of these bags to each sculpture – a white plastic carrier bag with a City of London crest and the name of the library. The tops of the bags have been sealed with packaging tape, so it's impossible for the purchaser to see what titles are inside. On the front of the bag there is a sticker that reads: "Mystery bag, a bag full of PBK's for two pounds, Adventure Category, please pay at the enquiry desk with correct change, thank you."

I secured an Adventure bag, two Romance bags, one Biography, one Science Fiction, one Travel, one Children's and one Crime. They were perfect. The instructions to the child were simple: the bag couldn't be opened but had to sit with the object when it was finished. By now you're probably frowning and confused. My reasoning for adding the bags was that if all the sculptures did all happen to end up the same, the bags would act as some sort of red-herring to the child, the spectator and myself. For the child in so far as acting as some form of obscure inspiration, for the spectator as a distraction, and to give me something new to look at and think about over the course of the following eight. My friend Adam comes to the studio around lunchtime with his son, Cosimo. Adam is an Art Insurer, involved in shipping, galleries and storage, which gets me thinking that Cosimo has probably seen a lot of art already in his short life. I guess he knows what it is supposed to look like. This is another flaw in the master-plan. It didn't occur to me until about the sixth sculpture that all the parents whose children I'd asked to borrow were, in fact, artists, gallerists or otherwise associated with the art world in some other way. I am evidently not a very consistent scientist. Anyway, Cosimo produced a beautiful abstract… thing, so I give him enough money to buy the complete Star Wars series on DVD. He told me he'd never seen any of them, and I found this so astonishing that I wanted to make sure he saw them in the correct order. He placed his bag of Romance next to the sculpture and I sent him on his way.

Alex and Tom (sorry), the same thing, some place, some time

There's a certain amount of fiction in my work. It's something I'm interested in and it's something that I manage to deal with, morally and ethically, because I'm making art which is not about 'the real'. It's about making conditions for other possibilities to exist… or so I keep telling myself. I have produced milestones from broken concrete from a Le Corbusier building in Marseilles that was really made by my dad in his garage in North Wales with B&Q cement mix. I have made a photograph of my family before me titled 'My family before me' (2006) that wasn't actually taken before I was born, I just wasn't there because I was in hospital. And I've had a crossword published in The Times containing a fictional word I invented, only it was really a single forged sheet printed with the same technique and wrapped around the real paper of that day. This is the nature of the production of conceptual art: the by-products are merely there to carry the idea. Did you ever think Cornelia Parker really sent that meteorite that landed in her garden back to space with NASA? Ever seen a photo or a letter? I doubt it, but right now, as you're reading this, there are maybe three or four people somewhere in the world sitting around a bar room table saying: "Did you hear about the artist who sent a meteorite back to space?" But that's not the really strange thing. The really strange thing is someone else somewhere else is also talking about it now! ... and someone else now! That is the work, and it wouldn't make it less of a thing if it never even existed in the first place, right? Sounds like I'm convincing myself, I know. Perhaps I am. I have another confession to make. Two of the children in the Rietveld experiment were fictional too. Even typing this now turns my stomach and fills me with dread because one of those sculptures by a fictional child was sold to a good friend of mine and I never told him. I think if I did tell him he probably wouldn't mind, but I don't feel the need to find out right now. The thing is, of course if I'm going to harp on about ethics and aesthetics, if I'm going to talk about values, then I should come clean and also admit that there was no conceptual reason for me to make two of the sculptures as if I were a young kid. The first one was made after a night of heavy drinking. I returned to my studio, where I was living at the time, and, under pressure from a gallery, I faked one that was due to be collected by FedEx the next morning. Bad man. The second was a quick- fix situation due to a child not turning up to produce the work at an opening. In the panic I constructed something in fifteen minutes around the back of the conference centre by a fire escape near the bins, so as to not be rumbled by the other galleries. These aren't even good reasons are they? Sorry Tom, sorry Alex.

A gallery, Amsterdam, The Netherlands, June 2006

A slightly shy but quite mature Dutch boy called, appropriately enough, Beer, began the construction process slowly and thoughtfully. Six people were present at the construction of the sculpture. Myself, actively helping to build the work and, then at some distance in the same room, his mother (the gallerist) and three other gallery staff. Beer spoke some English, which was good as my Dutch is atrocious, though I tried to make an effort by muttering lines from television commercials that had been drummed into me, to make him laugh: "Red Bull geeft je vleugels!" I'm not aware at what point exactly young Beer made a choice between form and function, but there most definitely was a point that everyone in the gallery acknowledged. The sculpture started as the others did, haphazard, free and without objective, but as the object took form, silence fell across the gallery and glances were exchanged. No one spoke for fear it would ruin what was happening, but we all simultaneously moved closer and closer in, forming a small pocket watching wide-eyed as Beer reconstructed a deconstructed Rietveld chair back into a Rietveld chair. I think I broke the silence first, but managed to wait until there were only three more planks remaining: "He's gone and made a Rietveld!" Of course the chair was not a precise replica – it was short of a few pieces because a small desk had been made too – but the resemblance was unmistakable. Even the incline of the back mimicked the angle of the original. I asked Beer's mother if he had ever seen a real Rietveld chair, or whether she knew if they had been taught about Rietveld in school. She was pretty certain he hadn't. On completion, Beer tried out his new workstation, and as he sat there proudly it crossed my mind that the look on that innocent child's face was not exactly one of pride, but instead of smugness – smugness for cheating me! I began to hate him and his stupid fucking chair and in a moment of paranoia I began to wonder whether he had been tipped off, and who exactly had put him up to it.

An artist's studio, London, UK, January 2007

A few weeks ago I read an article in the NME I really liked about some unknown band from Yorkshire. At some point the writer suggested that: "northern folk model themselves on the things they hate, rather than the things they like." Apart from it being ridiculously stereotypical and although this statement suggests that we northern folk come with an inherent air of negativity and bitterness, I do like the idea of evolving as a person knowing what you definitely don't want to be, rather than wanting to be like something else. That way you don't know where you are going, so it's much easier to get lost, like with this 'Faux-Modernist' chip I'm carrying around on my shoulder. By now I've become happily resigned to my so-called experiment. As such, it wasn't a very good idea to start with, and if I'd have proved my thesis, so what? I could start all over again, try harder, not intervene, keep control, and refuse to be swayed by external pressures... but in the end the ethics just aren't there.

PYJAMA BOTTOMS AND UGGS

A pair of pyjama bottoms emblazoned with the infamous 'I ♥ NY' logo, displayed alongside a pair of classic beige sheepskin Ugg boots.

Have you ever worn your pyjamas in public? Recently, whilst perusing a national British tabloid on the tube, I encountered an article on the introduction of a rule that forbids customers to wear their pyjamas whilst shopping in supermarkets, introduced by the national supermarket monopoly that is Tesco. Wrongly assumed to be a wildly unusual and infrequent event (unless driving to the hospital in labour or collecting milk from your front porch), venturing outdoors in nightwear has become increasingly popular in contemporary British culture. The forces behind the rule to ban the activity claimed hygiene as their motivation. I can't imagine bedbugs infesting the lettuce and such like, most likely it makes the stores look overly casual and, for other customers, it oozes 'chavdom'. Wearing pyjamas in public suggests: "I can't be arsed to get dressed". It's a signifier for those who got out of bed and are in need of a box of PG tips, a pint of milk and a packet of B&H to consume in front of an hour or two of daytime TV on the sofa.

The infamous Ugg boots, invented in Australia in the early 1970s, have similar socio-cultural values as Juicy Couture velvet jogging suits, grey sweatshirt jogging bottoms tucked into socks or oversized nylon American football team shirts with very short, brightly coloured, nylon running shorts (it is important that the shirt covers the running shorts so it appears that, when worn by young women, they are wearing no pants). Ugg boots announce, visually and symbolically: "This is me, this is what I wear, I don't care, I am comfy, I am off duty, I am happy. This is me." Perfect to combine with pyjamas in public therefore.

Almost a decade ago a similar trend could be seen on the streets of Manhattan. For entirely different reasons, the phenomenon of wearing one's pyjamas in New York City (with a woollen jumper or sweatshirt) signifies another purposeful announcement of class. There's an NYC phrase to describe the population who migrate to Manhattan in the morning and exodus in the evening: 'bridge and tunnel'. The Manhattan population swells by 87% in the day, and the privileged few that have the financial ability to live there use the rather derogatory term 'bridge and tunnel' to identify the commuters who live in the boroughs of Brooklyn, the Bronx, Long Island, Queens and Staten Island. On trains travelling to and from the boroughs young women wear pyjama bottoms, trainers and sweatshirts. The act of wearing pyjama bottoms whilst sipping a cappuccino in a Starbucks in Greenwich Village shouts: "I live upstairs and I've just nipped down for a coffee: I am one of the privileged who can afford to live on Manhattan. New York is my city and Manhattan is my playground."

A Nokia 6303i Classic mobile telephone with a newly recorded ringtone commissioned by the artist, that is an interpretation by a classical guitarist of the original Nokia ringtone known as 'Gran Vals', composed by Francisco Tárrega in 1902.

RINGTONE

Recently, as a sort of cultural experiment, I produced a personalised ringtone for my phone that is a reincarnation of the original Nokia ringtone, played by a classical guitarist. Originally the idea was related to the production of a new artwork, but it failed, as many do; a good thing as mistakes should be made and discarded.

The most frequently played melody in the history of the world to date is one played by default. The melody is commonly known as the 'Nokia ringtone' and is the default ringtone on all new Nokia phones, many of which are never changed to a personalised ringtone. This tune, that Nokia claims as an aural trademark of the company, first appeared on the Nokia 2110, released in 1994. It is estimated that the tune is heard 1.8 billion times a day across the globe, that's about 20 times a second. A mind-boggling statistic, though when dissected is relational to the fact that the Nokia ringtone is played numerous times in any one call, depending on how long the user lets the phone ring before answering it. It seems ironic that Nokia has expressed concern regarding copyright issues in relation to 'their' ringtone, as the tune was stolen from someone who couldn't defend himself nor earn royalties from its usage as he was dead. The Nokia ringtone was originally composed by Francisco Tárrega in 1902, titled 'Gran Vals'. Nokia found a loophole to make their plagiarism permissible by changing a single note. In Tárrega's 'Gran Vals', the final 'A' is two octaves lower than in the Nokia version.

To my mind copyright and the protection of a singular concept is for those who suffer from a lack of ideas. Fear of plagiarism is a concern held by those who have one or two good ideas in their lifetime; creative entrepreneurs and inventors who have daily flurries of ideas instead worry about editing their ideas down into those that should be developed and those that should be discarded. I am reminded of a song by Martin Creed's band, Owada, entitled 'Circle', a 2 minute 45 second melody containing a chorus as follows:

Stephen Willats thought that
Art & Language were ripping him off
Art & Language thought that
Joseph Kosuth was ripping them off
Joseth Kosuth thought that
Lawrence Weiner was ripping him off
on a recent trip to London
Lawrence Weiner saw a show by Stephen Willats
he said fuck me this guy's ripping me off[1]

1. 'Circle' by Owada from the album *Nothing* (1997).

I often listen to it and it reminds me that I should not worry about precedence or plagiarism. The McClintock Effect (the phenomenon of co-habiting women's menstrual synchronisation over time) has parallels in the conception of artworks in art schools, studio complexes, gallery stables and wider movements of contemporary art. "The thing about contemporary art is that nothing exists in isolation."[2]

2. Liam Gillick, from a lost radio interview with Martin Vincent, ill remembered by the author, circa 1999.

PERSONALISED NUMBER PLATES

UK personalised vehicle number plates displaying the registration BE5T DAD in the custom typeface Shanghai.

I happily admit to my disdain for personalised number plates. To me, the notion that an individual can pay a premium for a selection of numbers and letters, which only provide a scrambled meaning that the driver wishes to display on the front and rear of their vehicle, is a little incomprehensible. Drivers, after all, have the ability to produce a self-adhesive vinyl or any other form of signage to display on their vehicle. These would not only be almost free of cost, but would also produce an exacting message with as many characters as desired in any chosen typeface.

Personalised number plates are frequently a variation of the name of the driver (5AM or JENN1E for examples, or even T0M 1, T0M 2 and T0M 3 for each of his cars). Does that mean that without it owners would not be able to find their car in a car park? Is it because they find it too difficult to remember a seven figured license number? These number plates that identify the owner, and hence some sort of economic showiness, we can call 'class plates'. These types of plates adorn the cars of the aspiring middle classes. Drivers that wish to communicate to other road users the great heights of their social stratification, and in turn the importance of their presence on the road. They are signs of self-worth and self-importance. These personalised plates do not adorn the cars of those with true wealth, who usually wish to remain anonymous. 'Class plates' are purchased and displayed by the nouveau riche; individuals who wish to spend their income on signifiers that show a wealth that is merely aspired to. Class plumage and pretension are central to the idea of the detestable 'class plate'.

Less often, though still too frequently, personalised number plates correspond to a characteristic related to the owner's personality: BE5T DAD, HA5 BEER, WE11 JEL, or S3XY G4L. These cryptograms act as an individual's choice of clothes would, wittingly keying people into an understanding, whether it be true or not, of the driver's personality traits, or rather the traits that the driver would like to communicate to other road users. We can call these types of plates 'personality plates'.

The third type of personalised number plate we can identify as 'soul plates'; ones that are gifted from loved ones and are often invisible to other road users. Due to the nature of their invisibility these types of number plates are usually quite cheap and, therefore, less of an extravagance and more a mark of love, nostalgia or affection. An example of this type of number plate would be L3 JPH. On first glance it is a standard plate licensed to a car produced in 1993, however, when presented on a brand new vehicle it becomes apparent that the plate has been chosen personally. In this example the last three characters JPH are the only ones of significance, representing the initials of the car's owner Jacqueline Patricia Harrison, let's say. The L3 is the unwanted excess that makes the plate cheaper and less of a luxury. We can refer to these as 'soul plates' precisely because of their camouflaged nature or lack of visibility. The intent is affection not showiness and they lack financial value.

Perhaps more wondrously irritating than the personalised number plate itself is the personalised number plate typeface. In fact, in the UK it is illegal to alter the typeface of a number plate from the one specified in British road law, as it may confuse one's ability to recognise a vehicle's license number, and/or purposefully adapts characters to appear reminiscent of a different character for the sake of a personal reading. A good example of this is the numerical figure '1', which is often adapted with a forward or reverse pointing tail to resemble the characters 'L' or 'J'. The most popular of the personalised number plate typefaces come from variations on Western Roman character sets, which are then executed in an Eastern Asian manner, making the alphabetical characters seem more reminiscent of a Chinese, Japanese or Korean character set. A collision that is visibly nauseating.[1] This type of Eastern Asian number plate is stereotypically popular with testos-

1. This trend is also often observed in contemporary off-the-peg tattoos, the sociological cause and implications of which are brilliantly mind blowing.

terone-fuelled urban males who drive customised hot hatches with oversized, coloured alloy wheels. The cars are adorned with a variety of paraphernalia – purchased from Halfords – ranging from deafening chrome exhaust pipe expanders and window-tint foils, through to bullet hole stickers and a variety of signage that suggests the driver actually drives in an occasional rally. This decoration of a vehicle is more in tune with socio-cultural storytelling than presenting financial or economic signifiers. This signalling, when combined with a personalised number plate, leads to a thunderous barrage of the car owner's socio-economic and cultural position.

PAIRS

A wooden game of pairs produced by Atelier Fischer of Switzerland, with one tile missing, from the collection of the artist's daughter.

In the early days of my daughter's development – being a proud father with all the best intentions to buy her well-made toys that would contribute to her education and development – from my travels I would bring her handmade wooden games and objects; beautifully decorated, hand painted, and in perfectly chosen colours. This lasted for six months until she was old enough to express an opinion or at least a preference. It transpired that she preferred cheap, plastic toys, made in China, that you could find in British supermarkets. As opposed to spinning tops and rattles from Japan; xylophones from Scandinavia; maracas from Spain; Pinocchio dolls from Italy; model animals from Germany; or elaborate three-dimensional jigsaw puzzles of landscapes from Australia.

Instead, everywhere she went 'Tesco Baby' went with her, nestled under her right arm. It was as if the £2.99 replica baby, eyes permanently open, giving it a frightening fixed stare, was the most important thing in her small, but ever-broadening world. At the same time my daughter received Tesco Baby I also bought her a wooden box containing a game of pairs (alternatively known as the memory game) made by Atelier Fischer of Switzerland.

It was made up of 32 wooden tiles, each containing an image; the objective of the game being to find two matching images from an arrangement of all the tiles placed face down on a table. I have produced several variations of memory games and games of pairs in my own work over the last ten years, so admittedly this may have contributed to my choice.

It is interesting to me that these two toys, purchased at the same time, from very different contexts, with vastly different values and vastly different objectives, were in competition with one another. And that Tesco Baby inevitably won. I think I may have played with the pairs game more than my daughter. I only recently noticed that the game has a missing tile. It must have been pushed down a gap between the lounge floorboards, in my daughter's early inability to comprehend the difference between posting a letter in her toy letter box and posting a tile into the deep, unattainable abyss that are the foundations of our house. The remaining tile with the fat yellow duck is of course one of a pair of tiles that, without the missing one, is defunct.

STAB VEST

A very limited edition body-warmer, produced by Moncler and designed by Pharrell Williams to mimic the appearance of a stab vest or bullet-proof jacket, secretly given to the artist by the fashion editor of a well-known magazine. The artist is unable to wear the vest due to the dubious nature of its acquisition as well as the dangers associated with tempting fate.

There's a Moncler body-warmer that I'd seen in print, but was certain I'd never see in reality. Designed by Pharrell Williams, the body-warmer mimics the look of a stab-proof vest or a bullet-proof jacket, an anomaly in the history of fashion design. This garment is highly desirable: firstly its provenance – manufactured by one of the most prestigious, well-crafted and expensive ski brands worldwide, Moncler (founded in 1952 by French entrepreneur René Ramillon), and designed by Pharrell Williams, the multi-talented American rapper, singer, record producer, composer and fashion designer. Secondly, Moncler limited the production of the vest to an incredibly low number, meaning that the value has become incredibly high. I very proudly own one of these garments, and for the first three months after acquiring it I talked about it at every possible opportunity. When I was in Amsterdam last year (by chance collaborating on the production of a custom pair of

G-Star denim jeans) a fashion editor of a well-known architecture, fashion, design and lifestyle magazine mentioned the Pharrell/Moncler garment to me. I told him that if the opportunity ever arose I would purchase the body-warmer at any cost. A couple of weeks later a package arrived at my studio by motorcycle courier from the headquarters of the magazine. Inside was the body-warmer with a note: “Don't wear this on television or in media type situations as I'm pretty certain you are not supposed to have it. X”

At this point the tale turns sour; the first thing I did was check the label: size small. The vest did not fit. Searching on the internet, I discovered the vest was only made in a small size. The size of Pharrell Williams, its main user and model (but aren't most hip-hop stars big fellas?). With my brilliant tailoring skills – learnt from my mother who was obsessed with 1970s arts and crafts – I sewed an extension panel with a strip of Velcro where the vest naturally fastened at the side. It was tight, but it fit... The first time I put it on, I felt a million dollars and I took it out for a test drive. My studio is situated off Hoxton Street, an area in London that is predominantly a large council estate suffering from gun crime and stabbings. I went to the carpet shop. It was about six minutes into the walk that I began to wonder if it was a good idea. By the time I got to the carpet shop I'd had four 'street yoots'[1] point at me and two mumbled comments from passersby. The man in the carpet shop asked: "Why you wearin' a stab-proof vest?" I curtly replied: "It's a body warmer." As I left the shop I took it off and made my way back to the studio, slightly less warm, but in slightly less danger.

The problem with this body-warmer is that you can't wear it, because it's tempting fate. What if someone was to test it with a knife or a gun? Or even just a sharp pencil? I wouldn't be prising the compacted bullet out of the Kevlar-shielded midsection of a vest, I'd be having it surgically removed from my body, along with a handful of duck down. It's fine if you're on stage, at a photo shoot, in a nightclub surrounded by bodyguards or even, for that matter, at a VIP pool party at an art fair, but the reality of wearing a faux bullet-proof vest is more complex.

1. Young people (i.e. 'youths'). The phrase 'yoot' was coined in the film *My Cousin Vinny* (1992) in which protagonist, Vincent Gambini, played by Joe Pesci, pronounces 'youth' as 'yoot', due to his heavy New York accent. (Source: www.urbandictionary.com)

WIRE BENDING

A series of bent-wire miniatures illustrating various trust-exercise poses. The miniatures have been produced by homeless people who bend wire into shapes for money.

DOCTOR, FEMALE, AGE 33
USE: Amusement
COST: £2.99 (though depends on the scale)
FUNCTION: Thought provoking
WORTH: Depends who wants it
AUTHORSHIP: Who made it
OWNERSHIP: To whom it belongs
REPRESENTS: Trust

CHEF, MALE, AGE 37
USE: Decorative wheelbarrow men
COST: Fifteen quid (sixty in Chelsea)
FUNCTION: Coat hangers
WORTH: Keeping forever
AUTHORSHIP: Arts and craft market stall holder
OWNERSHIP: Mine
REPRESENTS: Something to remember

STUDENT, MALE, AGE 21
USE: Mobile phone holder
COST: £5-10 depending on where it's sold?
FUNCTION: Useless ornament representing trust
WORTH: Wire is very cheap, probably cost 50p to make one

AUTHORSHIP: Wire bending street vendor
OWNERSHIP: The first wire bending street vendor to make one
REPRESENTS: Society's material need for useless novelty items

TEACHER, FEMALE, AGE 29
USE: Demonstration
COST: ?
FUNCTION: Illustration
WORTH: ?
AUTHORSHIP: Ongoing
OWNERSHIP: Shared
REPRESENTS: Support

FURNITURE DESIGNER, MALE, AGE 49
USE: Thought
COST: 99p
FUNCTION: Educational
WORTH: A small fortune
AUTHORSHIP: Ryan Gander
OWNERSHIP: Ryan Gander
REPRESENTS: Germany holding up Greece?

ROPE LADDER

A handmade rope ladder in a satchel, produced by the artist at the age of 21 as an art student in Manchester.

I made this ladder many years ago as an art student in Manchester. I had never visualised it as an artwork in a gallery setting, I made it and then, not knowing how to show it to people, I carried it around for a couple of weeks. It's not a very successful artwork; if we question it using the yardsticks by which we question most things we don't understand (function, use, cost, worth, value, ownership and authorship) we are left with very few answers. But, in all its illogic, I remember loving having it with me. The idea of being prepared in someway, like a survivalist grabbing their 'go-bag' at the first sense of a tremor preluding an earthquake. I also loved getting it out to show people and experiencing their reactions, partly because I couldn't use it, as I can't walk.

However, the real discovery (or rather logical realisation) I made in those weeks carrying the rope ladder, was that the object's function was poignantly singular: it was limited to being a tool for escape. The user had to be at the top to attach the ladder's hook to an anchor point and then descend. It revealed itself as a getaway device.

FUTURE SHOCK

Future Shock, written by the futurist Alvin Toffler in 1970, a book gifted to the artist by his father for his twelfth birthday.

On my twelfth birthday my father gave me a present that at the time seemed unusual, but which has subsequently identified itself as having been vital to my development and my intellectual understanding of inspiration. The book, written by Alvin Toffler in 1970, entitled *Future Shock*, was a presumptuous and, from today's perspective, naïve attempt to predict the future. My father purchased and read the book when he lived in the US during the summer of love, 1969, a year that I know helped define him as a person and was influential on his future. At the time I'm sure *Future Shock* was both an intellectual and ambitious attempt at social anthropology and futurology. Re-reading it now the predictions seem immature and obvious.

The funny thing about hindsight is its privileged position: until you reach its great heights the prospect of laser guns, teleportation devices, time machines and personal jetpacks becoming reality seems absolutely unimaginable. I remember when I first read *Future Shock* as a teenager, the excitement that pumped through my body as I pondered the merging of countries and continents, probable changes to currency and denominations – whether it was technological, political, geographic or behavioural – the idea of change excited me beyond bounds. The shock of the future is perhaps not the possibilities of what could be… but with the privilege of hindsight, the actualities of what wasn't.

TIN CAN MUG

A recreation of a mug encountered in the administrative offices of the National Centre for Contemporary Art and National School of Fine Arts at The Villa Arson, Nice, France.

During my days studying art in Manchester I was told by one of my tutors, a great man called Jonathan Callan, that in some senses everyone was an artist. The comment was made during a conversation on the subject of the innate human urge to be creative. His argument came from the perspective that creativity is the defining factor that separates us from the rest of the animal kingdom; that our ability to solve problems, make mistakes, learn from mistakes and experiment with diverse and seemingly illogical methods, is what humans have over other species. I find it difficult to understand ideas when described in a generalised philosophical manner, so I asked my tutor to give me an example. It was a wonderfully elegant one, which I use when speaking to students now: “If you were to give ten different people – chosen at random from around the world – a broom and asked them to sweep a wood workshop, you would find that everyone brushed the room in a totally different manner. Some would brush all the sawdust into the middle and then collect and dispose of it in a bin bag; others would brush from the wall furthest from the door in the most direct line towards the door and brush it over the step then collect it into a bag; others would brush towards one wall and then down one wall; whilst others would brush illogically and less economically." [1]

I think in the majority of creative and problem solving acts, beautiful and magical things happen, more often through accidents, making mistakes and compromising, than from the basic dualities of cause and effect, supply and demand or problem and solution. In my tutor's example, the most illogical way of sweeping the room may in fact have sparked a discovery in the field of pattern making or enabled the sweeper to find a solution to another problem entirely. Sometimes the long way round allows us to stumble across things that are inconceivable at the outset of a task.

A few years ago I found a tin can mug in the offices of a Museum in Nice, in the south of France. A humble object which, on first sight, struck me with its ingenious use of materials. The (now rusty) can was used to hold pens on an office desk, but was clearly designed as a mug for a hot beverage. It had had a length of plastic-coated thick electrical wire wrapped around its top and bottom and joined on one side to form a handle (necessary for drinking hot beverages). Though it struck me as brilliant, in many respects it was also unfathomable; the primary function clearly being to hold hot drinks, but why would the designer have chosen a material

1. Not the exact words of Jonathan Callan, my memory and too many years may have distorted this passage.

that would rust and had a razor sharp rim unsuitable for drinking from? It occurred to me recently that the mug was a profit of circumstance: someone with an active imagination presented with two materials – the tin can and the length of wire. The mug is a good example of ingenuity, mistake making and problem solving. I've thought about it often since I first saw it and recently contacted a curator at the museum to see if it was still there. Luckily I had a photograph as it had been thrown away. I set about making a replica. The problem now is that I'm not sure what to do with it. I suppose it will make a good pot to put my pens in.

BLACKBOARD

A worn blackboard, originally used as a tableside menu, appropriated from a Lyonnais bistro.

There is a beauty to the French bistro single blackboard as a tableside restaurant menu. It is simple, economical, adjustable and logical. It probably existed in the first ever kitchen to produce food for money in France, and has not changed since. And why should it? If it serves a purpose and the purpose does not evolve, why should it change?

The French bistro tableside blackboard menu purports the logic of fresh food. It is a 'from soil to plate' mindset, in which we find an increasing obsession. It is important to understand the imperative behind this blackboard, in opposition to numerous printed menus. In a traditional French bistro, food is cooked and served until it runs out; food running out is a signifier of freshness and local provenance – there are no mass quantities stored in freezers to cater for endless customers. I've never seen such a menu (which is usually delivered and exhibited balanced on a rickety old chair at the side of your table) without at least one dish struck through with a line of chalk or wiped away with a damp rag. In a British restaurant it might be frowned upon if a number of dishes, or even one dish, on the menu was not available. Seen instead as a mark of disorganisation and inadequacy, though it's just as well really, as the time taken to strike through unavailable dishes from every printed menu would be utterly uneconomical. The different understandings of unavailable dishes between the two cultures is vaguely amusing.

The French bistro menus are battered with worn down corners and surfaces grey with the dust of thousands of erased menus. Adorned with French schoolgirl handwriting, immaculately executed curls and swirls with no uppercase. It's an aesthetic that I actually find vaguely nauseating; steeped in romanticism and childhood nostalgia for Isabelle, a childhood romance and lost love. Handwriting that oozes with the clichés of everything French, a pastiche.[1] Cliché or not, the genius of the blackboard remains, but the blackboard that is burnt into my memory exists in the background of a grainy black and white George Brassaï photograph: a beautiful young couple kissing at an outdoor bistro table, glasses of red wine, Gauloises lit, black turtleneck jumper, he carries a camera.[2] Isn't every experience in France, in Paris, just like this? Barthes suggests that the best place to view Paris is from the Eiffel Tower, precisely because from the Eiffel Tower one cannot see the Eiffel Tower and therefore is not reminded of the mawkish pastiche that is the picture perfect ideology of Paris.[3] "Why did the Englishman go up the Eiffel Tower?" "To get an eye-full of Paris!" Probably not to confirm the image burnt into his retina by the thousands of postcards for sale on the terrace opposite Rue Beaubourg.

1. It seems astonishing that the two words – cliché and pastiche – that can most adequately represent my understanding of French culture, Paris in particular, both originate from the French language and their etymology is relatively direct.

2. Yes, we see a camera, through the lens of a camera, carried as a prop rather than a tool. We are made aware of his capability of capturing this moment, reinforcing and immortalising the very same cliché.

3. Roland Barthes, *The Eiffel Tower and Other Mythologies*, Hill & Wang (1979).

A five-person, seven-day survival kit especially suited to use following an earthquake, containing, among other items, a chemical toilet as well as earthquake slippers with reinforced soles which enable the wearer to escape over broken glass and other dangerous terrain.

I recently came across a survival kit in the Japanese department store Tokyu Hands and, although it was costly, I found it impossible to turn my back on it, so I ordered one to be mailed to the studio in London. I've had an obsession with being prepared since childhood, the pragmatic boy scout in me reasoned various 'what if' scenarios, which mingled with images of me piling the family and the 'go-bag' into the car in the event of a large-scale natural disaster. More importantly, I wanted the articles in the kit to recreate the Tokyu Hands display, to remind me of an idea that had passed through my mind when I saw it: the notion of a modern still life. The survival kit, containing a multitude of items, varying in size, shape and colour, had been displayed in a way that only a Japanese department store dresser could achieve. Exquisite. The display was staged on the end of an aisle in a prominent location (it being shortly after the disastrous Miyagi earthquake) and had an air of tranquillity about it. Every item was perfectly considered and placed according to unfathomable rules of line, form and shape, as if a higher being with exceptional aesthetic mastery had produced the arrangement. Such care, patience and consideration. It reminded me of Ikebana, the Buddhist art of flower arranging introduced to Japan around the 7th century, a spiritual act that must be performed in silence.

It always occurs to me when I see a historical still life painting that the objects have an abandoned, haphazardness to their positioning, despite the obvious attention to detail paid to make it just so. Though most art historians would argue for the overriding importance of symbolism in still life paintings I think that it is secondary, or at least at odds, to the aesthetically pleasing qualities of the arrangements. Fruit, flowers, bounties of game, pebbles, skulls, candles and scrolls – in many still life works the choice of objects are arbitrary, merely material to be used in a ritual of placement. In many respects the display of the survival kit is a perfect image, it has an air of a photographic test display about it. These test displays are used to test photographic film and digital image sensors' abilities to capture tone, colour, detail, texture and line and often incorporate colour charts, wine bottles, brightly coloured cuddly toys, Rubik's Cubes, monochromatic eye-charts and such like. They are selected in a way that the camera can capture the full range of its capabilities. The day the survival kit arrived from Japan I unpacked it excitedly, taking care not to destroy any of the packaging needed in the display. I went about setting it up as I remembered it. Ikebana is significantly harder than it looks.

EAMES OTTOMAN

A Vitra Ottoman designed by Charles and Ray Eames in 1956, shown here in the newly introduced extra large size, with its corner sawn off.

Buying an Eames Lounge Chair and Ottoman today you will be given a choice of two sizes: standard or extra large. Standard has the original dimensions designed by Charles and Ray Eames released in 1956. The extra large version of this design classic was introduced in 2010 by Vitra, the only manufacturer legally licensed to make and sell Eames furniture. The need for an extra large size became apparent as numbers of customers in the late 1990s and early 2000s complained that the headrest on the chair was too short for the length of their bodies. Vitra's official statement regarding the introduction of the new extra large size states that it is a result of the evolution of human dimensions, rather than a rectification of a fault in the initial Eames design.

Can the average shape of the human figure change so significantly over a period as short as 30 years? After a little amateur detective work, it transpired that in the past 40 years the width and girth of the average American body has increased rather than the height. It seems plausible that the extra large version of the Eames Lounge Chair and Ottoman has been produced for a new obese American market. I am continually shocked at the width of wheelchairs used by the ground staff in American airports in comparison to European counterparts. I've always imagined that human physical evolution happened over a matter of centuries rather than mere decades. I remember recently watching a television program stating that the average position of women's nipples had lowered over 3 cm on average during the past 50 years. Again very plausible; in vintage porn it's astonishing how models have such upwardly pointing, ski-sloped breasts. Only in the last decade red squirrels have become brown squirrels that have bred with grey squirrels that have made aggressive black squirrels; our thumbs have become longer and more agile (probably through mobile phone usage and text messaging); and our earlobes have become increasingly elongated. Cats become lazier and dogs become more stupid. All is in flux. If you come across television commercials from 1960s America you find quintessential English accents selling you Cross Your Heart Bras or Pears soap. One hundred years ago there was no American accent as we know it today, merely a brutal concoction or amalgamation of a surprisingly diverse array of bastardised English. The most convincing of which (or the one most likely to successfully sell you a bra or a bar of soap) was the Queen's English. Actors such as John Wayne who featured in Western Films throughout the last century, playing the characters of homestead settlers, cowboys and cattle ranchers, address one another in a very stereotypical John Wayne-esque accent – an American English. But in reality a cowboy from the 1870s would most likely have spoken German, Dutch or Spanish. Realising the sheer youth of the United States of America, as a country, is dazzling, as dazzling as its lack of cultural history.

Richard Sennet suggests that the American grid system used in city planning was a strategy subconsciously related to guilt.[1] In every other society the layouts of modern cities are based around historical landmarks, routes, tracks, boundaries and geographical features. Why does every American city not reinforce the history that was there before the white settlers? The grid could be considered a zero point, a nullification of all the history of the Native American, cancelling it out and wiping the slate clean so that modern Americans would not feel guiltily, reminded of a heritage that their ancestors destroyed. Conjure this image in your mind, if you will: Charles Eames in 2070 reclining on an extra extra extra large Eames Lounge Chair and Ottoman, dwarfed by its enormity, in his hand is a controller for a PS12, on the holographic screen that miraculously floats in front of his eyes we watch him play a futuristic incarnation of the game Sim City. The game is a retro re-release of a version from 2012; Eames builds a settlement called Venice Beach placing buildings in a grid formation and in an immaculate straight line along a curving shoreline.

1. Richard Sennett, *The Conscience of the Eye: The Design and Social Life of Cities*, Faber and Faber, 1991.

A model, scaled-down for the purposes of visualisation, of a work by the artist based on the moment Sol LeWitt conceived his incomplete cube series, which is said to have begun as a scratching post for his cats.

There is an art world fable that I've heard on a number of occasions. I've been told it by Nicholas Logsdail, founder of the gallery I work with in London, and by his son, Alex, a gallery director I work with closely. Although the two accounts differ in parts, both Nicholas and Alex heard the story from the artist Dan Graham, who heard it from a friend of Sol LeWitt, who heard it from LeWitt himself. The story goes that a friend entered a young Sol LeWitt's apartment, which at the time also acted as his studio. LeWitt, owning two cats, had cobbled together a scratching post-cum-climbing frame to keep his two felines entertained. It was made from 1 × 1 inch timbers and consisted of a square on the floor to create stability, one vertical post, and then a 'L' shape that was attached horizontally to the vertical post. String was wrapped around the timbers for the cats to claw at. The friend approached the scratching post and announced to LeWitt that he thought it was a wonderful work and asked if he planned to make others. Surprised and amazed, LeWitt hastily replied: "Yes of course, it's a new series I'm working on." The friend left and LeWitt went about turning the scratching post into a series of incomplete cube sculptures, which he continued producing for the following two decades.

Storytelling is accountable for much of the advance in civilisation, with technological and agricultural knowledge passed on generationally through time. I take delight in the spaces of miscommunication and misunderstanding in storytelling, the ways in which meanings evolve and exaggerate into different things altogether. Imagine if all the knowledge of mankind as it stands today is the result of a huge string of misinterpretations: if every tale, song, rhyme, fable, poem and folklore was the result of an expanded game of Exquisite Corpse, or Chinese Whispers.

On a recent trip to New York I found myself introduced to the daughter of Sol LeWitt at a gallery opening, I could not muster the courage to ask her if the story was true for the fear of being disillusioned. I hold that tale of LeWitt's artistic development very dearly, like a lucky mascot. My father says you should never let the truth get in the way of a good story, I think it's the best advice he has ever given me.

A well-travelled and well-worn Rimowa Topas Cabin Multiwheel IATA aluminium suitcase, fastened shut with two TSA locks.

The Rimowa suitcase is a wonderful symbol of the truly globalised citizen. It tells tales of decadent explorations and is a social crutch or psychological support whilst travelling through a mass of nonspace and foreignness. The movements of the Rimowa suitcase mime the movements of the traveller: from home to cab; from cab to airport; wheeled through airport; to luggage belt; to ground staff vehicle; to conveyor belt; to aeroplane hold; the flight; to conveyor belt; to ground staff vehicle; to luggage belt; to owner; wheeled through airport; into cab; from cab to hotel. An extension of the traveller themself.

The suitcase is a transportable package, a home from home containing the bare necessities, belongings, and signifiers of a personality. Our obsession with packing is well catered for – we are overloaded with in-flight magazine questionnaires about what to take where and packing strategies (such as spreading your belongings on your bed, taking away half and then packing). Images abound on Flickr's pages showing travellers accounting for the contents of their bags and documentation is rife of reat explorers' equipment being dragged on sleds to the South Pole or hauled on backs across the Himalayas.

The aluminium Topas Cabin Multiwheel IATA Rimowa suitcase has been designed not just for any traveller, but for the traveller who wants to appear truly global and truly well-travelled. The dimensions of this particular Rimowa are the exact size of an aeroplane's overhead locker and is identified as such by the International Air Transport Association. In terms of luggage capacity, this is the most economical and perfectly conceived suitcase. It also fastens shut with two TSA (Transport Security Association) locks which means that this piece of luggage will never be forced open at customs because customs officers around the world have the key to be able to open it without destroying the locks. The battered, well-worn outer shell containing the remnants of barcode luggage labels, security stickers, elastic bands from travel tags, and the straps from broken off upper-class membership travel cards, speak of aspiration for all that is jet-set; for all that is global.

AUBETTE ASHTRAY

A redesign of an ashtray for Café Aubette originally made by Theo van Doesburg in 1927, from the perspective that van Doesburg and Piet Mondrian never met.

I'd seen the Aubette ashtray in books for years, but encountering it physically, by chance at Tate Modern in the show *Van Doesburg and the International Avant-Garde*, was a massive surprise. It was almost as if I had always thought it had not existed in the real world, like a prop in a film or a play. With Georges Vantongerloo, Jean Arp and Sophie Tæuber, Theo van Doesburg designed the decoration for Café Aubette in Strasbourg – a large restaurant with a cinema and dancehalls.

Mondrian and van Doesburg were the best of friends for 20 years or so. They would see each other daily and write to one another when they were living in different cities. Mondrian made paintings using colour field planes between horizontal and vertical divisions, making abstract compositions. He had an aversion, even a phobia, to the dynamic aspects of a diagonal line. Van Doesburg, I think, although they were friends, was taking the piss – repeating Mondrian's efforts at a 45° angle. I prefer the work of van Doesburg to Mondrian massively, mainly because he seemed to be planting a conceptual twist as opposed to making abstract paintings. He was taking what

Mondrian had already achieved, and wryly, boldly recycling it. After 20 years of friendship the pair had a falling out over a stained glass window with numerous diagonals in it, devised by van Doesburg. The two never spoke to each other again. It's not like one of them slept with the other one's wife, it was over a diagonal line. Last year I redesigned the ashtray for Café Aubette, from the perspective that van Doesburg and Mondrian had never met. It looks like this.

BUMPER BULLY

An American consumer product called a Bumper Bully. The rubber mat is fixed to the rear bumper of an automobile to protect its bodywork from damage in minor collisions, usually when parking or in slow-moving traffic.

As an American invention, the Bumper Bully is a familiar sight in the USA, especially in the West Coast cities, where congestion is acute but the vastness of urban sprawl makes it necessary for everyone to have a car to enable them to get around. I remember being awestruck when I first saw this object, not because it was out of the ordinary to me, which it was, but because it instantly communicated the offensive psyche of its user. A defensive mentality is always needed to navigate a city of pedestrians, cyclists and other road users, but the Bumper Bully clearly encourages aggressive behaviour. It allows the user to feel protected enough to be courageous beyond their usual capabilities. Comparable to that of the stab-vest or a bulletproof jacket worn on the body, the Bumper Bully has the same false sense of bravery,[1] the consequence of which is a hostile and belligerent road user.

1. Similarly in extreme sports such as rock climbing, the dangerously heroic edge that comes with the knowledge that, what is usually a solitary act, is being observed, photographed, videoed or even broadcast live via the internet is known as 'Kodak Courage'.

RYANAIR BOX

An empty cardboard box produced by the budget airline Ryanair solely to illustrate the volume of positive space available to their customers to store hand luggage in overhead lockers once aboard their aircraft.

The names of individuals in this text have been changed to maintain anonymity.

On 18 April 2012, at 14:50, Barnie Page wrote:

>

Dear Sir or Madam,
I am emailing you from the studio of British artist Ryan Gander. Ryan has an exhibition in September of this year at the Palais de Tokyo museum in Paris. For this exhibition he is showing a collection of design objects that he finds intriguing. One of these objects is a Ryanair cardboard box that is used to show passengers the size and weight limit for carry-on luggage. I called customer services and the ground team and they gave me the email address for Stephen Jackson as they said he might be able to help. I emailed him but I got an auto-responder saying my email had been deleted. I was wondering if you might be able to help?

I look forward to hearing from you!

Best, Barnie Page

>>>>>>>>>>>>>>>>>>>>>>>>>>

On 19 Apr 2012, at 16:00, Robin Watson wrote:

>

Hi Barnie,

We can arrange to have a box left for your collection at one of our London airports under the condition that a £100 donation is made to a charity of our choice.

Could you send me on more details of the event?

Thanks, Robin

>>>>>>>>>>>>>>>>>>>>>>>>>>

On 20 April 2012, at 15:20, Barnie Page wrote:

>

Hi Robin,

That is very kind of you, and we would be happy to make a donation. The exhibition is called Ampersand and will take place at the Palais de Tokyo from September to December 2012. The exhibition will consist of classic design objects and other items of interesting design, each item selected has an anecdotal back-story by Ryan and is somehow associated with at least one other item in the exhibition. I don't know much about the stories but I know that alongside the Ryanair luggage size box will be a well-used and well-travelled Rimowa suitcase, which is the exact dimensions permitted as carry-on luggage. The items in the exhibition are to be displayed on a conveyor belt and viewed through a window so that only one item is visible at a time, sort of like the generation game!

Palais de Tokyo opened in 1937 and is now the biggest and best regarded museum dedicated to modern and contemporary art in Paris. It has recently undergone huge refurbishment but is re-opening tonight in fact! It is a huge honour for Ryan to be asked to put on an exhibition there. Would it be possible for us to collect the box from Gatwick airport please? As this is probably the easiest airport for us to get to.

Best, Barnie

>>>>>>>>>>>>>>>>>>>>>>>>>>>

On 20 Apr 2012, at 16:34, Robin Watson wrote:

>

It shouldn't be a problem. If you want to get in touch closer to when you need to collect the box and I'll organise it for you.

Thanks, Robin

>>>>>>>>>>>>>>>>>>>>>>>>>>>

On 20 April 2012, at 16:35, Barnie Page wrote:

>

Thanks very much Robin,

I'll speak to Ryan on Tuesday and figure out a good time and then I'll let you know.

Best, Barnie

>>>>>>>>>>>>>>>>>>>>>>>>>>>

On 23 May 2012, at 15:59, Robin Watson wrote:

>

Hi Barnie,

The request has been further reviewed and unfortunately we no longer wish to be involved.

Best of luck with the exhibition.

Kind regards, Robin

>>>>>>>>>>>>>>>>>>>>>>>>>>

On 23 May 2012, at 16:10, Barnie Page wrote:

>

Hi Robin,

I don't understand what has changed? It's an integral part of the exhibition and the item it will showed alongside (Rimowa suitcase) has already been purchased at great expense, and will be rendered useless without the Ryanair box beside it.

I would be most grateful if you could review this decision!

Best, Barnie

>>>>>>>>>>>>>>>>>>>>>>>>>>

On 23 May 2012, at 16:49, Stephen Jackson wrote:

>

Dear Barnie

We have concerns over the design rights of the box and its graphics, and the potential for pilferage from our bases if it becomes a 'design object' in the exhibition so we have to decline.

I am very sorry and wish you all the best.

Regards

Stephen Jackson

Head of Communications

>>>>>>>>>>>>>>>>>>>>>>>>>>>>

On 23 May 2012, at 17:12, Barnie Page wrote:

>

Hi Stephen,

That's a huge shame and it will really make a large dent in the concept of the exhibition as well as the exhibition itself. The catalogue and text for the exhibition has already gone to print so it's going to be embarrassing for us (and probably for Ryanair too) when people ask questions about an object described but not actually on display in the exhibition. It's also a shame for Ryanair that an object with your logo on it won't be shown in this exhibition by a world-renowned artist in a very highly regarded museum. I suppose our correspondence will make for an interesting appendix in future editions of the accompanying publication.

Regards, Barnie

>>>>>>>>>>>>>>>>>>>>>>>>>>>>

OYSTER WAND

A customised wand with an electromagnetic chip removed from a Transport for London issued Oyster payment card attached to one end.

My brother Neil once explained to me an idea he had for producing an entertaining, performative way of paying for transport within London. The existing method of payment is the use of a Transport for London Oyster Card. The card contains a tiny microchip with an electromagnetic antenna that runs around the interior of the card, meaning it can be touched on swipe pads to receive or make payments. Neil's idea was to remove the tiny chip from the card and superglue it to the end of a toy magic wand. When approaching a swipe pad on any form of London transport it would then be possible to make the wand appear from one's sleeve as if by magic and tap the swipe pad with the tip of the magic wand, miraculously instructing it to show a green light and allowing you to pass. Brilliant. A true crowd pleaser to brighten the days of the grey haze of London commuters. There is a beauty in this display of currency; if the money has to be spent anyway, why not creatively increase the value-for-money and provide positive fulfilment for other citizens for the same cost?

There is a pub, local to where I have lived in London for the last ten years. It's called the Golden Heart and I go there occasionally. The landlady,

Sandra, is the most wonderful character you could hope to meet. She has been there for 35 years and has watched the local area change rapidly and dynamically over that time. The pub is situated in Spitalfields, presently a very fashionable area, mainly frequented by people from the creative quarter: a sea of tight jeans, thick rimmed specs, and pointy silver shoes. Spitalfields is also on the cusp of The City of London, which is populated by young, wealthy, aspiring businessmen, hedge fund investors and bankers, whose nihilistic approach to life astonishes me. There is friction between the two camps, which are separated by one single street.

Over the last decade I have countless times observed groups of 'banker wankers' roam into the Golden Heart with their aggressive, sarcastic, egocentric, bullish wealth and disgruntle not only the locals and the young creatives who frequent the pub, but also the staff and its owner Sandra. Many times I have seen Sandra sending them away, suggesting they are on the wrong side of the market and that there are a number of cocktail bars across the street where they might find a more appropriate atmosphere. One time, before Sandra had the opportunity to turn one such group away, I observed a more sinister ritual of the city workers. They played a game, preluded by a chant, at the end of which they pulled out their wallets and each took out a wad of £20 notes. These were then counted, out loud, in front of the group and all else in earshot. It lasted a while as they were all carrying cash in the region of £400 – £600. There wasn't a winner in the game, only a loser. The banker with the least cash, as a forfeit, had to buy the next round of beers. A round that might have come to £15 at most.

In many respects this display of wealth is the opposite of my brother's idea for the Oyster Card magic wand. There is a part of me that feels a project coming on, but first I'm going to have to do some research into the amount of currency an Oyster Card microchip can actually hold…

BLACK DRAWN CURTAIN

A black velvet curtain, which one might associate with the theatre or cinema, suspended from a circular rail. The curtain is drawn shut to conceal a space within.

There's not much I can tell you about what is behind the curtain, but maybe that's the point. Or maybe the point is that it's the curtain you should be thinking about, not what it's concealing. The decision to present you with a drawn curtain is not to deceive you or to aggravate you. It's not an elitist gesture intended to isolate you from those in the know. It's more generous to present the curtain closed rather than open. Closed, the curtain represents everything and anything, a vessel for backstories that shoot off in spastic tangents, reaching the far-flung edges of history, science, poetry, medicine, love... Destinations that are immeasurable. Depending on how well honed your imagination is, we can go anywhere from here, whilst those whose imaginations are a little more flabby will probably justify their frustration with rejection.

THE SITTING

A self-published book of questions, tasks and directions usually assigned by the artist on the occasion of a conceptual portrait commission, to be completed by the sitter prior to the production of a portrait. The copy on display has been completed by the artist himself, making it suitable material for the production of a self-portrait.

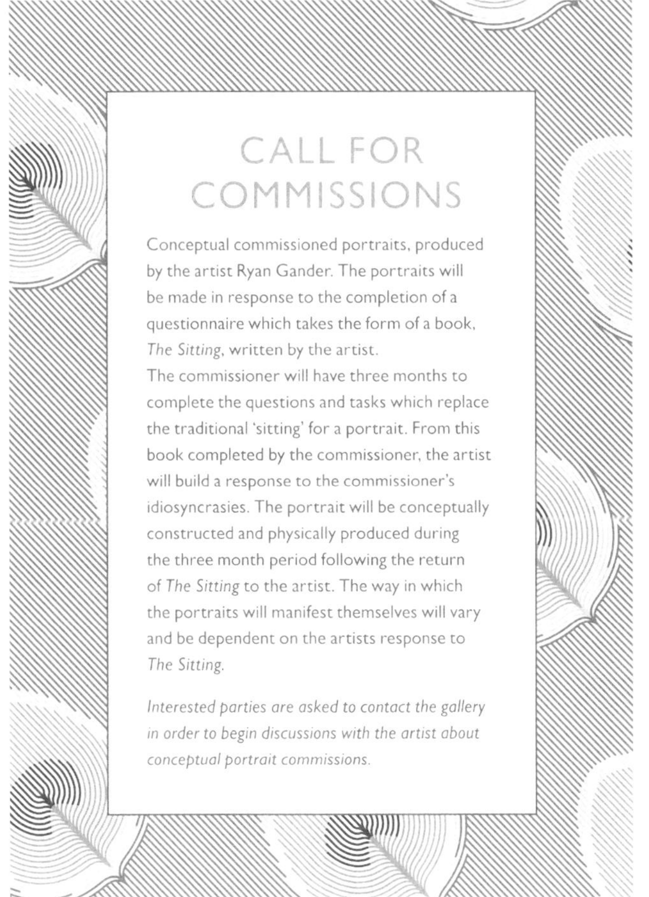

CALL FOR COMMISSIONS

Conceptual commissioned portraits, produced by the artist Ryan Gander. The portraits will be made in response to the completion of a questionnaire which takes the form of a book, *The Sitting*, written by the artist.
The commissioner will have three months to complete the questions and tasks which replace the traditional 'sitting' for a portrait. From this book completed by the commissioner, the artist will build a response to the commissioner's idiosyncrasies. The portrait will be conceptually constructed and physically produced during the three month period following the return of *The Sitting* to the artist. The way in which the portraits will manifest themselves will vary and be dependent on the artists response to *The Sitting*.

Interested parties are asked to contact the gallery in order to begin discussions with the artist about conceptual portrait commissions.

ROLEX

Two reproductions of the artist's black wristwatch produced by Rolex and customised by Bamford, originally acquired from an art collector's wrist in Tokyo, in exchange for a sculpture. Each replica is displayed in a Plexiglas display case, one 300% larger by volume than the other to illustrate the difference in spiritual and intellectual value of one identical object to another, due to their histories and backstories.

As an artist I meet a host of collectors from all over the world, and often we have little in common. I have a small, pokey and inexpensive personal collection of art myself, which is simply not comparable to a true collector's collection, so that doesn't act as fodder for conversation. Now and again circumstances bring me across a collector who I instantly relate to and who fills me with interest, intrigue and aspiration. Masamichi Katayama is a prime example. If he had not been a collector – let alone of my work – and we had met, I know we would have struck up a rapport. Katayama is a brilliant man, who I am in awe of, and proud to call my friend.

Katayama is a very well known interior designer (frequently appearing on television in Japan), though in my opinion he is more of a creative entrepreneur, dipping his finger into a vast array of pursuits from clothing to interior design, collecting, publishing, teaching… the list is endless. He has worked on a massive number of projects including A Bathing Ape stores around the world; Mackintosh in London; Ozone, the highest bar in the world at the 118th floor of the Ritz-Carlton Hotel in Kowloon; the Nike Harajuku in Tokyo; and the Uniqlo on Broadway in New York. Katayama's art collection is mainly housed in his self-designed, self-built offices in Shibuya-ku, Tokyo, where I am seriously honoured to have my work entirely occupy the ground floor.

Recently I saw Katayama at the opening reception for an exhibition in Tokyo, and through a translator he said that he would like to purchase a work in the show. The work was a large sculpture, 'It smells like darkness - (Alchemy Box #26)' (2011) in the form of a locked Parisian book-vendor's stall. Inside were books, each one chosen by one of the artists who had previously shown in the gallery, enabling it to approximate a time capsule for the history of the institution. Naturally I was really happy Katayama wanted it, of course for the income, but also because such large works are so much harder to sell (big sculptures + unsold + returning to fester in art storage = an expensive equation). Katayama acquiring the work for his personal collection would mean income and fewer storage outgoings in the future. Double, double good.

Since I had known Katayama I had eyed his

watch that always adorned his left wrist. He'd told me the provenance: a Rolex Daytona, customised by Bamford of London so that the entire watch was black, made in an edition of 25 (and which was sold out immediately upon its release). With a price tag of £28,000, this was a watch that I could neither afford nor would ever in my lifetime purchase (no matter how much money I earned) because of the guilt associated with such extravagance. Slightly drunk, with a wry smile, I suggested to Katayama that we made an exchange: the sculpture for the watch. Incredulously he immediately released the strap and passed the watch to me. His translator relayed to me that it was a perfect swap. I was lost for words. On the way back to my hotel I began to feel uneasy about the exchange, not knowing whether Katayama had agreed because of a polite Japanese custom, or a genuine commitment. I wondered if he regretted it and I texted his translator suggesting that if Katayama wasn't happy he could get the watch back off me the following day. She replied: "He's fine, but he keeps looking at his bare wrist. Don't worry, we'll get him a new one." A little less guilt-stricken I placed the watch on my bedside table and woke countless times in the night to make sure it was still there. I had never owned anything as valuable and it wasn't insured.

Upon my return, Ann-Marie at my studio, with a mind like a fox, suggested we insure the watch as an artwork. By inserting it into the studio's database it would become insured with the other artworks and, as I would always wear it on my wrist, I would be the accompanying art conservator/transporter, meaning that the contractual obligations of the insurance for an artwork would be complete. Perfect. Sneaky. When Ann-Marie asked me for a title for the artwork the words: "Time is money, my friend" slipped off my tongue. This got me thinking. It got me thinking about currency, value, worth and cost. It got me thinking about art's ability to hold value, even in the chaotic and desperate times of a recession. It got me thinking that routinely, our faith or belief that currency equates to value, is scrutinised and renegotiated. In every society there are points at which people hold up a banknote and say: "What the fuck is going on? This is a piece of paper!" And, at moments in history when we lack faith in our monetary systems, the natural inclination is to return to a process of exchange, bartering for goods and services. There are both quantitative and qualitative values for everything, for example if I charged five pence a word for writing this particular text I would stand to make approximately £64, but what value does the text have if it is not interesting enough for anyone to read? There are objects and materials that have a logical and necessary value, such as food; there are totems, charms, wayside monuments etc., that represent belief in ideas; and there are decorative objects whose prime function is to aesthetically enrich our lives, but Art is a magical equation of both the aesthetic enrichment and the totem-esque signifier of belief, as well as status, taste and a host of other values.

My exchange with Katayama got me thinking about the value of art, and the value of my art in particular. I would hazard a guess that to those collectors with whom I have an affinity, the most prominent value system related to my work is in its storytelling. The works I make are vessels for back-stories, cultural collisions, ideas about para-possible histories and how those parallel histories may affect the world around us. The objects aren't really artworks as much as off-cuts, receipts or by-products of thinking. The thinking is in fact the artwork. The watch didn't become an artwork when Ann-Marie input the title 'Time is money, my friend' (2011) into the studio's database, nor when Katayama placed the watch in my hand. The Bamford Rolex that I wear on my wrist everyday is an artwork because it is a carrier or a motif of the story that I have just told. A story of an exchange between friends.[1]

1. In swapping his watch with me that night, Katayama facilitated the exchange of two artworks; 'It smells like darkness - (Alchemy Box #26)' (2011) and, in addition, 'Time is money, my friend' (2011), the Rolex he gave me. Although I retain authorship of the artwork, in many respects it is a collaborative work. Just as I record the story here in written text, I am sure it comes to fruition in other places, on other occasions. Most likely whenever people that know him well ask him what happened to his black Bamford Rolex.

COLOURED TOILET PAPER

A stack of fifty-four toilet rolls, six each of black, red, green, blue, fuchsia, orange, yellow, purple and brown produced by the Portuguese company Renova.

I first encountered Renova toilet paper in a French supermarket, whilst on holiday with my family. I clearly remember the vivid colours displayed, coincidentally, on a high shelf just out of reach, as if the product was in some way illicit or there was guilt associated with its purchase, like pornographic magazines on the top shelf in newsagents. Various friends have admitted feeling embarrassed or ridiculous carrying toilet rolls home from the supermarket, particularly when that was their only purchase. We all need to shit, it's innate, but the image of a person walking home with twelve rolls of 3-ply, quilted, soft white under their arm makes our need to excrete loudly visible.

The aestheticisation of toilet roll is a curious phenomenon, largely because the user's interaction with it is so brief. Manufacturers' motivations towards the aesthetics of the bathroom seem sound; in the 1970s and 1980s pastel coloured toilet rolls prevailed, complementing the bathroom suites of a fleet of suburban housewives and bringing a sense of calm to their bathroom activities. The very existence of bright shades such as yellow, blue, green, purple, red, orange, brown, fuchsia and black is vaguely preposterous. The introduction of such vivid colours encourages us to view the toilet papers not as monochromatic planes, but as two tones: brown on brown, brown on black, brown on yellow, brown on fuchsia etc. The most sensible answer to the question of these colours must be economic and social; the buyer's intention in purchasing coloured toilet rolls is to suggest gratuitous luxury. Extra expense and lack of necessity places the buyer in a realm of pseudo-decadence, a realm of dinner party conversation fodder. Though wiping one's arse does not make pleasant dinner party tête-à-tête: "I simply love your bog roll!" "Thanks, isn't it fantastic? Have you tried the chocolate mousse?" The toilet is a personal domain where personal encounters take place. And after all, a handful of (soiled) black toilet roll disappears with a flush, as quickly as its soiler's shit.

MR PLAYLIST

A 9 carat gold 36GB USB drive containing a playlist of songs whose titles begin with 'Mr'.

Beep. A grey plastic key fob, looking not too dissimilar to a tiny mouse, is placed against a small plastic box of the same colour. A single LED blinks and then a huge iron gate that forms the only entrance to the compound slowly grinds its way open. This is how the Academist begins their day, unless of course they happened to have fallen asleep the previous night slumped over a table in their atelier, in which case they would have more than likely awoken to the morning chorus of the Rijksakademie cockerel or a screech from one of the five resident peacocks.

My atelier is situated in the Ménage. During a welcome tour with about 30 other participants from around the world we were informed by our guide that previously, almost a hundred years prior to our arrival, each of the workspaces in this section of the building were stables for the Dutch cavalry's horses. I say something ridiculous like: "It is comforting to know we'll be working in a stable environment!" attempting to break the ice. No one understands. Everyone looks back at me blankly. I feel really English. The floor is grey concrete, the walls are institutional white and the doors are mid-tone grey, obviously. My name is etched into a glass plate, riveted to the door just above the keyhole. The door is large. Large enough to get a decent sized horse through (whether it be cast or real) and it slides on runners from left to right. I close the door behind me and I find myself in a very large atelier. Two walls are exposed brick with large windows, the other two are white and the ceiling is suspended quite high and made from a transparent PVC type material. In the far corner is an enclosed booth with a grey lockable door leading within. It says in the welcome brochure that this is my office. Sickeningly it boasts broadband Internet connection, phone and fax. In addition, the office is sound and dust proofed from the rest of the studio. The office's scale is more to what I am accustomed for the size of a studio. I am not aware of it at this moment, but I will come to spend many hours in this room. The front wall of the office has a giant glass window that looks out onto the rest of the atelier; it's a bit like the type of thing you would expect to see in a recording studio. However, on the other side of the window there's no drum-kit or guitars, just a fearfully enormous empty white space that looks as if it would gobble up any attempt at art that I would endeavour to insert. That was my first day. The second and third day I filled by purchasing all those essentials from the Dutch equivalent of Pound Stretcher: pin-board, bulldog clips, four socket extension leads, mouse mat etc. The fourth, fifth and sixth day I busy myself with settling in and sitting in the cafeteria talking about 'important issues' with other participants. Every day during the following month seems quite similar. I arrive at the gate hellishly early (my middle-class, North of England work ethic still needs exorcising), then sit in my office drinking coffee. I check my email, I read and I make notes for most of the day, or compile useless playlists on my computer, songs whose titles have the word 'Mr' in them: Mr Wendal, Mr Brownstone, Mr Moustache, Mr X, Mr Tambourine Man, Mr Robinson's Quango, Mr Bojangles, Mr Blue Sky etc. Occasionally I glance up to see if my atelier is still there. And it is. And it doesn't change. In fact I only ever enter it en route to my office. Thirty days pass and I don't make anything. I suppress my guilt by telling myself that I am 'researching'. In addition to researching I am also becoming acutely aware of the atelier from inside my fish-tank-type office. I am slowly beginning to internalise it. That's why I can't start making anything yet. I am weighing up the space. It's as if, by looking at it, it's very slowly becoming a part of me, like a second skin. I have a fear of sounding as if I am describing the paranormal as I write this, don't get me wrong I am not some weird spiritual type, however something magical was happening inside that atelier. It seemed to be getting bigger! After the following 30 days there was no mistaking it, it was unarguably larger. Naturally, I couldn't mention any of this to my new peers, fearful that it would result in jealously and arguments over unfair distribution of space amongst the Academists. It was approximately three months into the residency that the others found the courage to make the first steps with their work, albeit small, a splash of paint here or an hour in the editing suit there. I was still sitting tight five months in, I hadn't touched anything related to the production of art for almost half a year and it was terrifying me. Maybe the problem was that I had left it too long. Of course by this time my atelier was at least ten times the size of most of the other participants' and making something within those four walls would be an immeasurable task. My studio had grown and with it had my fear. It had become impossible to make anything. How could anything I make live up to the conditions in which it had been produced, and after all, what do you make when you can make absolutely anything? One day during my sixth month it all ended quite simply. I arrived at my atelier, surprised to hear the sound of a Dutch radio station coming from behind the door. There were workmen inside installing a new central heating system. I was astonished to find that their presence had deflated my ateliers enormity. I made them some coffee, we sat and I briefly spoke about my dilemma with them and then I assisted them in fitting electrical gutting around the skirting board. The following day when they had moved on to my neighbour's studio, I went about cleaning up the debris they had left. I was puzzled to come across a blue and black fishing float with orange and yellow bands around it. I picked it up, examined it, then went across to the sink to wash it. On my way back from the sink I passed a door that was resting on two trestles to form a makeshift table. In the corner of this tabletop someone had drilled a tiny hole, only about 2 mm in diameter. I looked at the float in my hand and then automatically stuck the end of it in the table to see if it would fit. The moment I let go, I had finished my first work, 'Workspace Addition #1' (2001). The fishing float stayed sticking up from my table like a little aerial for the following year and a half. It wasn't the best thing I ever made but when I think back to it now, I wish I'd been brave enough to make some more mistakes like that.

QSL COLLECTION

A collection of thousands of QSL cards inherited by the artist on the death of his grandfather. Similar to a postcard, the QSL card served as written confirmation of a prior radio transmission, which was subsequently sent between the two radio operators by postal mail.

During the Second World War my grandfather, Frank Dunn, was a radio operator in the RAF as part of the crew of a Bristol Blenheim bomber plane. He was fluent in Morse code, it was in his blood, and for many years after the war he had an amateur radio set in the small spare room of his house, which he used to communicate with people all over the world. One of his objectives was to communicate with people in places he had never been able to contact before. This was also the main objective of a competition called The Worked All Britain Awards. The main aim was to make radio contact with someone and log their location by colouring in the corresponding grid sector on an Ordnance Survey Map. The more of the map you coloured in, the higher you scored. To confirm their contact, the communicating pair also sent each other a QSL card. It was ironic that he could talk to anyone, anywhere in the world for free, but then he would have to pay the postage of a postcard to confirm it. QSL cards are largely homemade by the radio operators themselves, who have no graphic or visual training, so naturally they are extremely beautiful and honest.

After losing a tiny, furry toy bumblebee given to me one Christmas as a child, I spent the following week looking for it, crying. Since then I have tried to train myself to become less emotionally attached to physical objects. I try not to associate objects with people and emotions, for fear of creating keepsakes that I might lose. It's as if the loss of an object, which is a connection to an emotion or person, is also the loss of that person or that emotional connection. I have a wedding ring, and although it represents my marriage to my wife, who I love very much, I keep an emotional attachment to it at arm's length, knowing that whether I lose it or not, I will still be married to her and still love her. My father has stones that he took from his father's grave at his funeral when he was just 15 years old. I remember my countless nights lying awake as a small boy worrying that one day he would lose them and would feel tormented by the loss.

My QSL collection is perhaps the most valuable thing I own; it is impossible to remove my emotional attachment to it because my grandfather left it to me in his will. Also, although the collection has no financial value, culturally it represents, what I believe to be, a hugely significant contribution to the landscape of unschooled graphic design, which is some of the best graphic design in existence. I feel like a custodian of a cultural currency, with my collection of historical worth that I must protect and preserve for future generations. The collection must be digitised and backed up, otherwise I will never sleep at night.

A Japanese table setting, made from various lacquered woods, earthenware and porcelains, for a traditional multi-course kaiseki ryōri banquet.

JAPANESE TABLE SETTING

On my frequent trips to Japan I am continually amazed, mesmerised and dumbfounded by the nature of the Japanese table setting. Its historical significance and storytelling abilities are widely unrealised by westerners. The kaiseki ryōri banquet originates from the 16th century referring to 'cuisine for a get-together' and today a kaiseki ryōri banquet incorporates the use of 16 or 17 different vessels and utensils per person, each vessel made from a different material. Various lacquered woods, earthenware and porcelains with different colouring, patterning and shaping all represent or comment on the dish they are designed to contain. The idea that dishes are designed and handcrafted with the food in mind is massively appealing to me. I've often wondered if it would be discourteous to serve a different food in a dish to that which was intended, almost as if the wrong union of a food and vessel could disrupt an invisible sorcery existing between master potter and master chef. As if compromising the intentions of craft could upset the balance between presentation and taste.

In *Empire of Signs*, Roland Barthes writes avidly of the table setting as an image:

The dinner tray seems a picture of the most delicate order: it is a frame containing, against a dark background, various objects (bowls, boxes, saucers, chopsticks, tiny piles of food, a little gray ginger, a few shreds of orange vegetable, a background of brown sauce), and since these containers and these bits of food are slight in quantity but numerous, it might be said that these trays fulfil the definition of a painting which, according to Piero della Francesca, "is merely a demonstration of surfaces and bodies becoming ever smaller or larger according to their term."[1]

1. Roland Barthes, *Empire of Signs*, Editions d'Art Albert Skira SA, 1970, p. 11.

In my mind, the courses of a traditional Japanese banquet are akin to a stop motion animation. Everything being played out, presented, perused, observed, tasted, commented on, frame by frame, moment by moment, course by course, dish by dish, over a long period of time, and most of all perhaps suggesting the banquet as a spectacle for participants.

One evening in Tokyo, during dinner at a friend's apartment, I was offered a simple dish comprising of a green bean salad with a sesame seed dressing. As the dish made its way across the table I commented on the beauty of the pot in which it was served – a shabby earthenware with some graphic markings in a shiny black glaze around its edge. The woman to my left quietly and shyly chuckled to herself, commenting that it was the host's favourite pot from a vast collection passed down from generation to generation. The pot was 800 years old, from Chinese descent, and was valued at £15,000 to £20,000 and yet it was still being used, which would be unheard of in an equivalent friend, apartment and social situation at home in the UK. Although the craft and the decoration of the pot were significant, the meaning of the pot and its capacity for carrying a story came foremost. The pot or vessel in Japanese culture is a functional object first and an aesthetic object or a signifier of status only secondly. The pot is devoid of meaning when it is not used; only a carrier of meaning and folklore as it is passed from person to person, around a table or eaten from, morsel by morsel.

THE REVERSE OF A SECURITY MIRROR

A circular convex security mirror with protective visor intended for outdoor use, manufactured in Japan, viewed from behind.

There are many examples in the history of art, of artworks that negate the reflective surface of a mirror[1], for example a mirror's reflective surface hung to face the wall. Although there are many precedents for this, the idea of inverted mirrors is interesting nonetheless. Obviously inverting a mirror renders it defunct, yet the object becomes more potent through potential or imagined belief as opposed to actual knowledge. Mirrors, after all, are made of glass with one side coated with foil, and glass is a transparent material through which we are invited to gaze from either side. There is also an intriguing dualism between "this is what I see" and "this is what you see" that exists in the pavilions of Dan Graham for example. However, I'm more interested in seeing the same object from many possible perspectives; the ability to see a single object from the front and reverse at exactly the same moment is as compulsive as it is impossible. Although it's an over-the-hill art school tutor's cliché to advise their students to turn the object upside down, inside out or back to front and draw it (along with "Make 100!" "Make it big!" or "Why don't you paint it that colour?"), there is some poignancy to this exercise. Especially in relation to a security mirror, a tool whose function is to look at the person who is not there.[2]

1. Works by Mauro Vignando, Stefan Brüggemann, Michelangelo Pistoletto... the list is bountiful.

2. As explained in the text 'Security Mirror'.

DECOMMISSIONED AK-47

A decommissioned Kalashnikov AK-47 assault rifle given to the artist by Jake and Dinos Chapman for the intended production of an artwork to be auctioned in aid of the charity Peace One Day.

I was given this machine gun by Jake and Dinos Chapman. The idea was that I used the decommissioned AK-47 assault rifle in any way I saw fit and that the resulting artwork would be exhibited in London, then auctioned in aid of Peace One Day. Unfortunately it became obvious that the AK-47 was best served here amongst these other objects and ideas, in the context of this collection.

The intellectual dilemma with the AK-47, or the Kalashnikov as it's sometimes known (named after its inventor), is that there is a contradiction in its being. It is in fact as repulsive as it is marvellous. In terms of thinking about the gun as a tool (without deliberating its end function) it can only be seen as a thing of excellence and it has the characteristics of an object that has contributed significantly to world history. Even though the AK-47 was invented over six decades ago, it is still the most popular choice of assault rifle on the planet and is still the most widely used today. It is approximated that over 100 million AK type rifles have been produced. Reasons for its popularity include low production costs, mechanical simplicity (making it a tool that can be easily maintained and repaired), simple design, compact size as well as the ease and speed of adaptation to mass production. It is also a tool that, like all important tools, can be easily modified by its end user for more specific functions. In fact, it has been estimated that there are no less than one hundred iterations and variants of the AK series including an AK sniper rifle, an AK shot gun, an AK grenade launcher, and an AK sub machine gun, as well as numerous designs for magazines and ammunition clips.

The making of the AK-47 is a difficult thing to celebrate. Perhaps our task as we gaze at this incredible object, is to separate the tool and the history and evolution of its design, from the fact that it is a weapon of murder and the history that comes with that occupation.

A variation of the artwork 'To Protect Taste' (2011) by Cory Arcangel, entitled 'Enjoy Responsibly' (2012) by the artist, consisting of a wastebasket filled with empty Bacardi Superior and Zero Calorie Cola cans.

The act of collecting centres around ownership for many people. This applies to stamps as much as it does to art. For other collectors the joy is in the act of finding, researching, hunting, and obtaining. Collections have their historical prize find, their most valuable piece, their rarest examples and their most nostalgic or sentimentally valued. I am a collector of objects with back-stories, some of which I find and some of which I make (handy as this is my occupation). A problem arises when objects I long to enter my collection are made by someone else and have the alchemic roles of being 'artworks'; unfortunately I don't usually have the means to purchase these. There is, however, one object in my collection that defies this, because I obtained permission from the artist to reproduce it as an 'example' of art.

'To Protect Taste' (2011), is by the artist Cory Arcangel, whom I hold in supremely high regard irrespective of our friendship. The work consists of a wastebasket filled with empty limited edition Tron Coke Zero cans. It exists and is available to buy as an artwork, but it's too expensive for me.

I explained this to Cory along with the fact that I didn't want the object as an artwork per se, but as an object for my collection of 'worldly stuff'. I really didn't expect him to spontaneously suggest I produce another one, not as an artwork, but as an 'example' of his work. Something for which I am indebted.[1] The Tron cans are so limited edition that I couldn't reproduce the work, so Cory, being easy-going Cory, suggested I choose other cans with the word 'zero' in the drink's name. I chose Bacardi Superior and Zero Calorie Cola cans, narrower and taller than a regular can and black with a gold top rim, which I mimicked on the rim of the black wastepaper basket that contains them. From Cory's directive the 'example' of a work is entitled 'Enjoy responsibly' (2012), after the slogan that appears on the can itself. The work is a beautiful example of an example of his work. Still, you have to wonder if it will ever be worth anything.

1. Which means that when he reads this he will note the word 'indebted', the phone will ring and he will ask me for an 'example' of an artwork of mine. And so he may.

Common things always end up telling stories, stories always end up having something in common.

This fifth edition is built as an open sheet of 'A4 Paper', a familiar surface on which to relate stories.

As the first edition of Roland Barthes' *Empire des signes* (1970) was composed in Albertina typeface (especially designed by the Monotype Corporation for Skira Editions, based on the sketches of Chris Brand), Ryan Gander's *Ampersand* (2012) is composed with a typeface called Empire – a revival of Albertina – created from observing how the letters, printed more than 40 years ago, have lost sharpness and detail and had new life breathed into them. Empire aims to give back to Albertina its own post-print story.

The cover incorporates the two colours, Bianchi Green and Hellelfenbein, from 'Spray Paint' and a typeface inspired by common british number plates, as referred to in 'Personalised Number Plates'.

The artist would like to thank:

Åbäke, Cory Arcangel, Nathalie Boutin, Jonathan Callan, Ashley Carr, Céline Chazalviel, Sébastien Clivaz, Elsa Delage, Frank and Eunice Dunn, Epic Fireworks, Europa, Ian and Frances Gander, Neil Gander, Olive May Gander, gb agency (Paris), Annet Gelink Gallery (Amsterdam), Laura Greening, Grizedale Arts, Frédéric Grossi, Solène Guillier, Gemma Holt, Ann-Marie James, Johnen Galerie (Berlin), Masamichi Katayama, Anna Ker, Lisson galerie (London/ Milan), Michael Marriott, Sarah Marston, Sébastien Martins, Rebecca May Marston, Phil Mayer, Akiko Miki, Spike Milligan, Jonathan Monk, Line Monthiers, Taro Nasu (Tokyo), John Henry Newton, Barnie Page, Toby Page, Peace One Day, Javier Rivero, Miranda Sawyer, Sébastien 'Rambo', Yumiko Shimizu, David Smith, Kajsa Ståhl, Anna Stoppa, Adam Sutherland, Maki Suzuki, Claire Szulc, the homeless of Hoxton, Tokyo Arts Club (Paris), Andrea Viliani and Rose Watkins-Jones, Felix Wentworth and T.E. White.